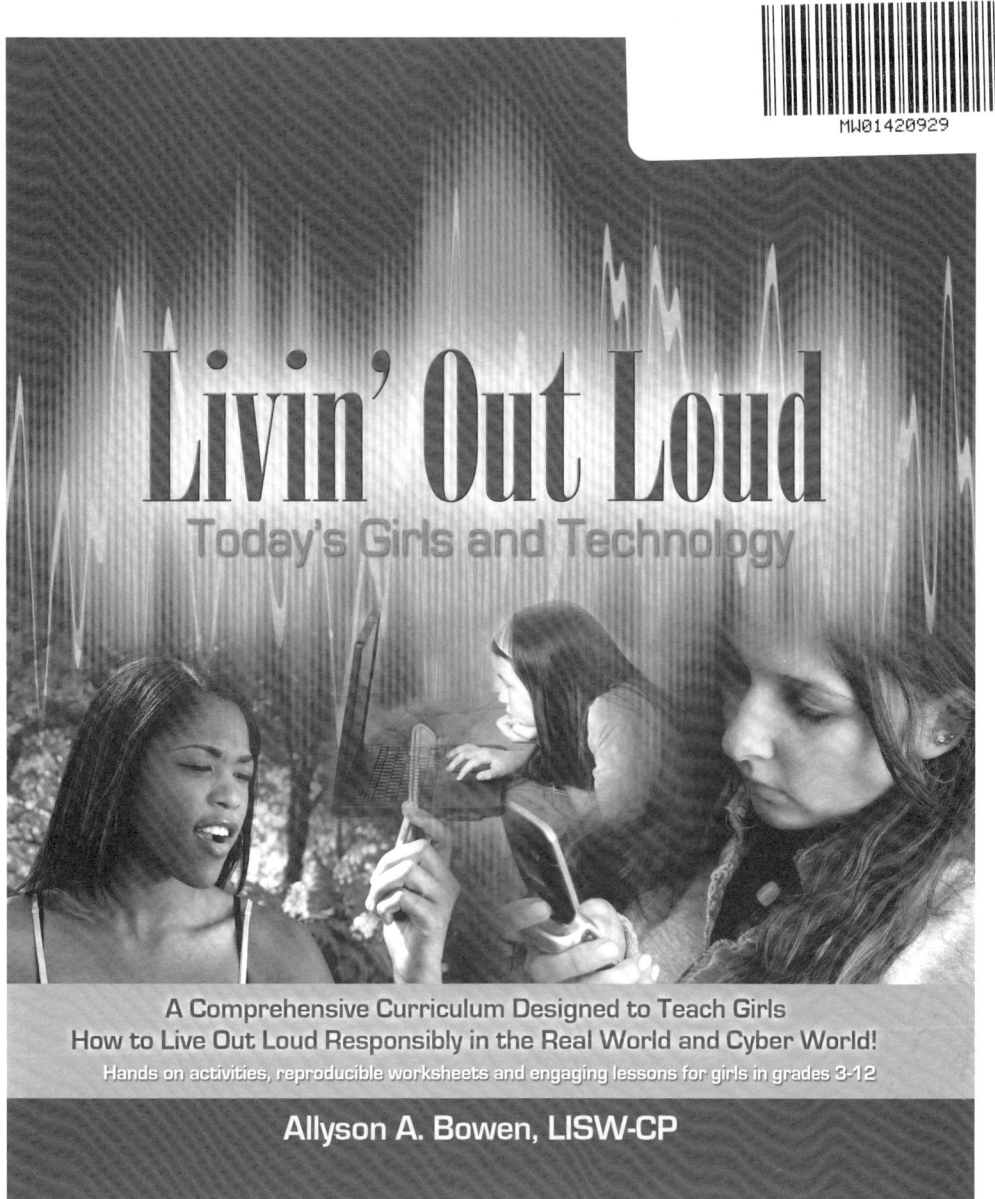

Moxie Girl Press
West Columbia, SC 29169
© 2009 Allyson Bowen, LISW-CP
www.be-love-do.com

All rights reserved.
Permission is given to reproduce the activities and worksheet
portions of this book. Reproduction of any other
material is strictly prohibited.

Art Direction and Graphic Design: Diane Florence
Editing: Misty Burton, Nicole Hold, Kaye Randall

ISBN 13: 978-0-61529-271-7
ISBN 10: 0615292712

Library of Congress Number
2009903951

Dedication

I dedicate this to all girls committed to working to make the sisterhood a safer place!

To all the role models who journey with our girls!

Acknowledgement

For His daily affirmation and guidance
of my dreams and ventures!

Our limited ability accents God's limitless power!
— unknown

To my precious boys! My husband and sweet son, thank you for your patience, encouragement and constant love...family love!

To my entire family who pray, support and encourage me. Thank you for your tremendous love!

Dear Facilitators,

Thank you so much for choosing the Livin' Out Loud curriculum. I hope you find this a fun and exciting journey for you and the girls in the group. I have tried to give you a variety of activities to choose from and trust that you will use your own creativity to add to each session to make it engaging and as exciting as possible. I hope you will laugh a lot while you are learning as I believe that is the best way!

Some of you may know my motto is **"Be a Moxie Girl!"** A Moxie Girl is one who came into this world to live out loud to her fullest! She is energetic, brave, courageous, determined, has heart and lot's of spunk among other things! My mission is to help girls (and guys too!) young and old find their Moxie!

I hope through this time together your girls will begin to discover who they were intended to be, have the courage to love with an open heart, and learn to do what it takes to make a difference. In the sisterhood and in our society we need to embrace differences, celebrate each other's gifts and talents and give back generously! There's no greater time than the present to get started!

I want to hear from you. If you have a story to tell or want to share an exciting group experience please visit my website www.be-love-do.com and click the link to email me! Thank you for being a part of making a difference in a girl's life! You inspire me!

With Moxie,

Allyson

Table of Contents

Introduction 7

Definitions and Facts 10

Statistics 13

Sexting 14

Activities 411 16

Inclusion: We all Belong 19

Current Mood 24

Livin' Out Loud 32

Face it: Fear, Fiction, Fact 35

Cyber World 41

Cyber Technology Crossword Puzzle 46

A-Z Power Me! Word Find 53

'I' Card 56

Avatar or Who you Are? 59

Me IRL (In Real Life) 62

Bullycide 64

She is... 66

Pieces of Me 72

© 2009 Allyson Bowen, LISW-CP

5

Table of Contents

Guess Who?..76

Mobile Me..93

Circle of Influence..96

Hi-5..99

Media Madness..101

Masterpiece..105

Acting Up!..107

When Pretty in Pink turns Mean and Green!..114

Kindness Cures 118

Healing the Hurt 122

I Will Never...126

Ready for Business 128

Appendix..135

Qualities, Strengths, Characteristics 136

National Volunteer Organizations 138

Livin' Out Loud Lessons Summary...140

References 143

About the Author 144

Introduction

There is no disputing that friends influence friends. It can be positive or negative but youth crave connections with each other. The need for acceptance, approval and belonging is vital during the adolescent/teen years. This is especially true for girls.

Girls have become creative in how they manipulate relationships to gain status and power. They maneuver so effortlessly their behavior has become almost stealth like. They use words as weapons, eyes for daggers and ostracize with ease. Depending on the role a girl may play in the social circle, she may be completely clueless to the abuse due to her desperate desire to stay connected. She needs to feel that she belongs to something bigger than herself. The impact of these behaviors may seem temporary but the power they pack may potentially have negative effects that could last a lifetime.

Indisputably, the mind and the body are related. When children and adolescents experience repeated highs and lows of emotions such as anxiety, anger, bullying and fear of rejection, they often fail to learn important social skills causing social isolation and lack of healthy connections within peer groups (Goleman, 2007).

This book will be about living, learning and loving; understanding relationships, facing fears, and acknowledging potential. Our girls today are in need of individuals who will journey with them to begin to discover all they were intended to be. Thank you for accepting the challenge!

The reality is girls today are Livin' Out Loud (LvOL) in a way that no one could have ever imagined. The girls we work with today were born into this technological age.

© 2009 Allyson Bowen, LISW-CP

Introduction

They do not remember type writers or even "bag phones." Hence they have sailed past us becoming so savvy that we are now scrambling to catch up and intervene to stop the cruel and sometimes deadly behaviors in this out of control world they are wandering through called Cyber-World!

Can we protect our girls in the real world and cyber world from the cruel intentions of others or from being the perpetrators of schemes and rumors? Maybe not completely but these behaviors are learned and therefore can be unlearned, there is hope! A 2005 Canadian study found that 80% of a child's socially aggressive behavior could be attributed to caregiver and peer influence (Brendgen et al., 2005). We can have an impact for change and early intervention is the key.

It is time we look seriously at what is taking place in girl world, recognize the urgency to intervene and place a poignant emphasis on changing how girls treat each other. We must provide the tools necessary and introduce them to trusted adults who know how to intercede to insure we do not lose another child to "Bullycide"! Bullycide is suicide caused by bullying (Marr & Field, 2001). The harsh reality is there are those who cannot take it any longer and choose to take their lives to end the suffering. Do not allow yourself or other faculty/staff members to dismiss how girls treat each other as "girls being girls" (this applies to "boys being boys" or "kids being kids" too!). Bullying is not a rite of passage; this attitude is the very essence of Bullycide!

Bullying behavior, at times, is allowed to thrive based on a lack of intervention. We must be vigilant in our efforts to stop the behavior when noted and

Introduction

communicate to them the behavior is unacceptable. Then we must educate and offer opportunities for reforming behavior. However, do not be misled that there are simple, one step easy solutions.

It is imperative there be a school-wide effort in addressing all types of bullying. Creating school norms is a crucial first step to success, establishing an environment where students feel safe, determining the bullying dynamic on campus and implementing procedures that are understood and enforced by all. Consistency and daily guidance is necessary as children and adolescents navigate the uncertainties of peer relationships, connections with others, and self discovery.

As human beings we are all created to connect therefore we must bridge the gap between ourselves and our students to cultivate the connection that is essential to thriving. We must work to promote relational justice and acceptance of others if we are to truly master the science of relationships, and help our girls embrace Livin' Out Loud!

Definitions and Facts

 ## RELATIONAL AGGRESSION

Relational Aggression (RA) is a term many have become familiar with in defining girl bullying. Do not be mistaken though boys can be relationally aggressive as well. Relational Aggression can be defined as covert bullying, psychological or emotional abuse intended to inflict harm in or among relationships (Simmons, 2002; Crick & Grotpeter, 1995). There are also two distinct characteristics of RA, an intent to harm and an imbalance of power. RA can be seen in all age groups from the very young to grown adults. Relational Aggression can also be very overt in nature such as blatantly excluding one through verbal or nonverbal messages or it can rear it's ugly head as rumors, gossip, eye-rolling, secrets or back stabbing.

 ## ELECTRONIC AGGRESSION OR CYBER BULLYING

Relational Aggression can also show up in cyber world. The term used is cyber bullying. Cyber bullying or Electronic Aggression is bullying behavior between peers where an individual is aggressively targeted, there is an imbalance of power and the behavior is repeated using digital technology such as computers or mobile phones. Cyber bullying can take place through instant messaging, mobile phones, text messaging, blogs, web sites, chat rooms or email (Aftab, 2006; Hertz & Ferdon, 2008; Kowalski et al., 2008). Parry Aftab, an internet safety lawyer and director of Wired Safety, one of the leading internet cyber bullying resources, states cyber bullying "... has to have a minor on both sides, or at least have been instigated by a minor against another minor."

Definitions and Facts

As in real world bullying, cyber bullying involves different roles that youth may engage in. There is a bully or perpetrator, a target and bystanders. It is important to use the term target and not victim. We have all been targeted and it is our ability to cope that prevents us from becoming a victim. The goal is to build resiliency and coping skills to prevent one from feeling like a victim. Everyone, at one time has been a bully, target or bystander and therefore it is important to educate about all roles.

It is crucial for schools to look at how cyber bullying is having an impact on their campuses. Determine if school policies and procedures on bullying address cyber bullying. Many times cyber bullying will take place off campus but could be a result of an incident that was instigated while in school. Schools must determine how they will address the situation when brought to the attention of faculty/staff or administrators. Being prepared will prevent ineffective reactions.

The war on cyber bullying is not only a school issue but a community issue. It is imperative to include parents and community leaders as a part of the comprehensive approach. Educating parents is an important step in supporting the efforts of the school. Hold community forums with local law enforcement and include information in parent handbooks concerning school policies and procedures in addressing bullying and cyber bullying.

The increase in popularity of the internet, instant messaging and mobile phones among adolescents and teens has catapulted cyber bullying to outrageous proportions and has unfortunately caught many off guard. Due to the swift rise of cyber bullying behaviors, legal professionals have found themselves reacting out of

Definitions and Facts

necessity to address this behavior with harsh and even at times criminal consequences. Many do not consider cyber bullying a criminal act however under many jurisdictions it is being addressed as a crime. It is important to investigate how your jurisdiction or province addresses cyber bullying.

Many states have created anti-bullying legislation and a few address electronic bullying or cyber bullying. To find out if your state has anti-bullying legislation visit www.bullypolice.org

Statistics

In 2004 the Centers for Disease Control reported that 5% of girls reported missing at least 1 day of school during a 30 day period due to safety concerns and 8% reported having been in a physical fight at least once in the previous 12 months.

IN 2006, A NATIONWIDE STUDY BY GIRLS INC. REVEALED THAT GIRLS FELT:

UNDER PRESSURE TO PLEASE EVERYONE 74%

STRESSED!
74% .... of High School Girls
56% .... of Middle School Girls
46% .... of Third-Fifth Grade Girls

SAD AND UNHAPPY!
42% .... of High School Girls
32% .... of Middle School
23% .... of Third-Fifth Grade Girls

WORRIED ABOUT APPEARANCE!
76% .... of High School girls
74% .... of Middle School Girls
54% .... of Third-Fifth Grade Girls

IN 2004, A NATIONAL LONGITUDINAL STUDY OF ADOLESCENT HEALTH STUDIED GIRLS IN GRADES 7 THROUGH 12 AND RESEARCHES FOUND:

- Girls were nearly twice as likely to think about suicide if they had only a few friends and felt isolated from their peers.

- Girls were more likely to consider suicide if their friends were not friends with each other.

- Girls who felt isolated and friendless were at as great a risk for considering suicide as girls who knew someone who had committed suicide.

- Research has shown that students randomly subjected to rejection experiences dramatically reduced IQ scores and made them more aggressive (Bearman & Moody, 2004).

© 2009 Allyson Bowen, LISW-CP

Sexting

One of the latest trends among teens is sexting. Sexting is when someone takes inappropriate or sexually revealing photos of themselves and sends it as a text message attachment. To our youth, sexting initially may seem harmless but in a flash the picture can be in the hands of thousands. When teens unknowingly disseminate the pictures to minors they have potentially committed a crime. Sexting in many states is a criminal offense and perpetrators must register as sex offenders.

IN A 2008 STUDY BY THE NATIONAL CAMPAIGN TO PREVENT TEEN AND UNPLANNED PREGNANCY AND COSMOGIRL.COM REVEALED:

- 22% of teen girls have sent nude or semi-nude photos of themselves

- 22% of teens admit that technology makes them personally more forward and aggressive

- 39% of teens have sent sexually suggestive text messages or email messages to someone

- 38% say exchanging sexy content makes dating or hooking up with others more likely

- 29% believe those exchanging sexy content are "expected" to date or hook up

- 66% of teen girls who sent or posted sexually suggestive content stated they did so to be "fun or flirtatious,"

© 2009 Allyson Bowen, LISW-CP

Sexting

- 52% did so as a "sexy present" for their boyfriend

- 40% sent pictures as a "joke."

- 75% of teens stated that sending sexually suggestive content "can have serious negative consequences" and 19% of teens say sending sexually suggestive content is "no big deal"

Sexting has proven to have grave consequences as in the death of 18 year old Jessica Logan from Ohio (Her teen committed suicide over "sexting"). The harassment, taunting and bullying she endured after an ex-boyfriend sent nude pictures of her to classmates led her to hang herself. Sadly, the decisions girls are making are ending in devastating consequences. We must tackle this serious issue to help our girls make smarter decisions and protect themselves.

ACTIVITIES 411:

The activities and strategies in the Livin' Out Loud (LvOL) curriculum address issues our girls are currently facing today in the real world and cyber world. LvOL was designed to be used with a small group consisting of 8-10 girls. If possible, the group intervention should be 10-12 weeks long. In addition, these lessons can be used as individual interventions.

This curriculum can be used in any setting involving girls and can be facilitated by anyone committed to helping girls. The activities are intended to educate, explore, gain insight and ultimately empower our girls to new awareness and action in their own life and in the lives of others.

As a general rule every activity will require a pen or pencil and other materials needed will be noted. The sessions should be an hour to an hour and a half. Each lesson will use the following format:

 WU: "What's Up" and "Current Mood," open discussion for each activity to "check in" with what's going on in their lives and identify their mood (current mood is explained in the "Current Mood" activity on page 24) This section will be conducted in the first 10-15 minutes.

 MSG: "Message" or objective of the activity

 Ne2H: "Need to Have" for the activity, such as other materials needed, or extra prep time for the activity

ACTIVITIES 411:

 CTA: "Call to Action" or procedure for the activity, other pertinent information. This section will be 30-45 minutes.

 LvOL: "Livin' Out Loud" practical application for daily emphasis and reminders for intentional living. This section will be the last 5-10 minutes.

The reality is many of our girls, especially by middle school and high school, are electronically connected and communicate using cyber world slang. To bridge the gap between our world and their world we will use some cyber world language in each activity.

As you begin to prepare for your group you may want to review a copy of the schools policies and procedures for addressing many of the behaviors we will discuss in the real world and cyber world to help your girls gain a perspective on possible consequences. If your school does not have policies and procedures addressing bullying and cyber bullying it would be recommended that a committee be formed to begin this process.

There are more activities included in the book than you will have time for in the 10-12 sessions. The activities are designed to be used with girls in grades 3-12 but you know the girls best so choose the activities that you feel will make the greatest impact for this group of girls. Most activities stand alone and are not in an order you must follow. However, the Current Mood activity is one you will want to do in the beginning as it is used as the opener for each of the subsequent activities. Have fun with this curriculum, be creative and add your own twist to the activities to meet the needs of the girls in the group. The possibilities are endless when we open our hearts to create change.

© 2009 Allyson Bowen, LISW-CP

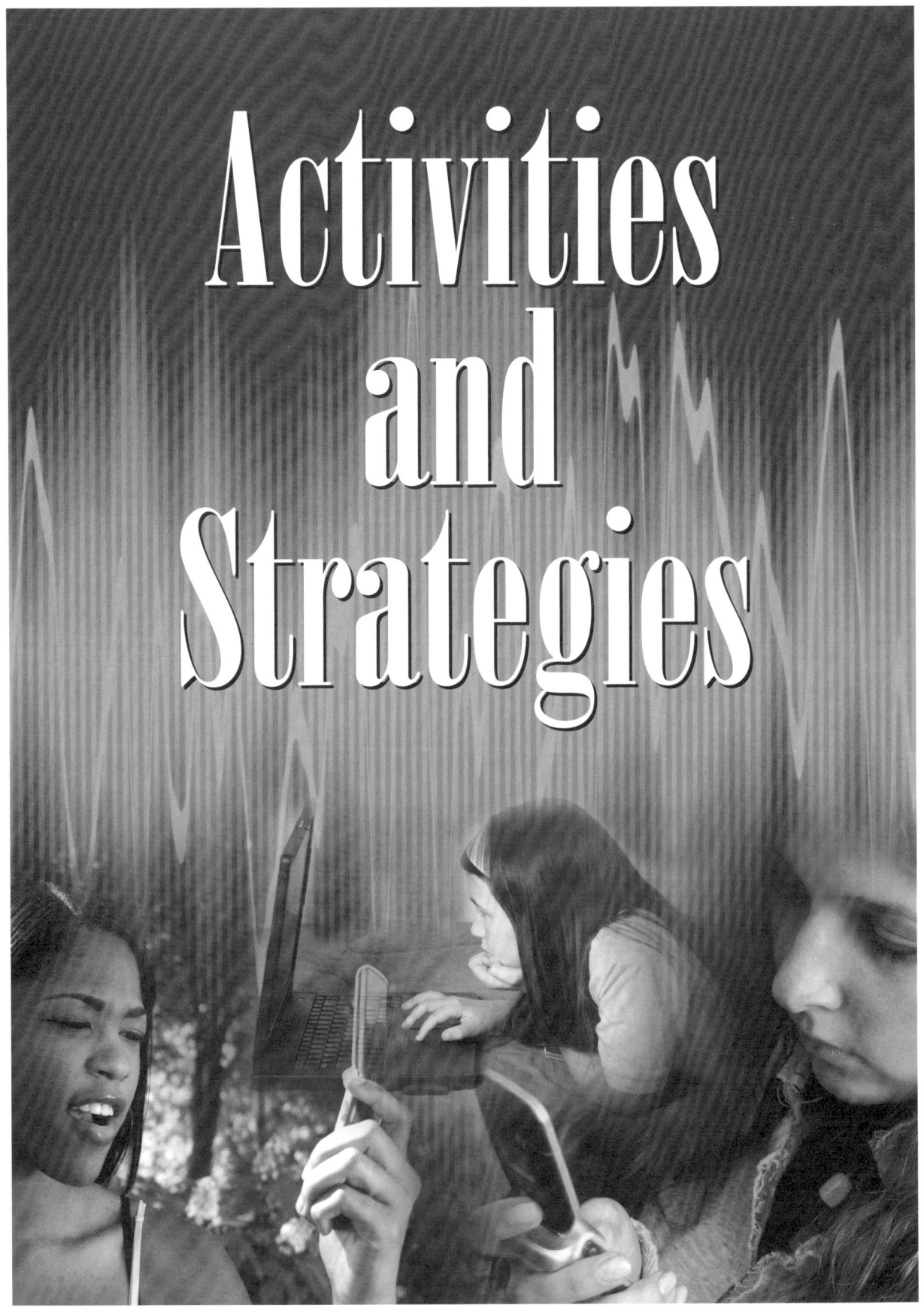

Inclusion: We all Belong

WU:
Welcome Activity: Getting to know each other Game

Ne2H:
Ring Pop Suckers
String
Conversation Card page 22

Getting to know each other game

Buy one "ring pop" sucker for each person in the group. Punch a hole in the top of the package and thread a string through it to make a necklace.

As the girls arrive place a necklace around their neck and give them one conversation card. Have them read the directions and as other girls arrive begin to complete the card. There's a catch! Inform them that they cannot use the word "I" until a designated time. If you use the word "I" and someone catches you, they get to take your necklace. This can get quite entertaining because when someone catches someone else, they usually blow it by saying, "I caught you!" or "I get your necklace!" or while looking to fill in the blanks on the conversation card someone will yell "I have green eyes"!

At the end of the time, give away a prize for the person with the most necklaces.

© 2009 Allyson Bowen, LISW-CP

Inclusion: We all Belong

Welcome:

Welcome everyone to the first Livin' Out Loud session. Hopefully everyone had fun playing the "ring pop" game and getting to meet the other girls in the group. The point of the game was to meet each other but it was also to emphasize that very small word "I." As a part of this group you will quickly learn the magnitude of such a very small word as you discover the individual you were created to be with many unique gifts and talents.

Our goal will be to learn how to LvOL Responsibly! Everyone here will hopefully discover their platform to stand boldly upon and announce to the world "I came to Live Out Loud!"

However, to gain the attention, acceptance and power you desire you must learn to LvOL with respect, character, integrity and an openness to always be willing to learn, grow and embrace change.

Once you have completed your welcome move into the second half of the activity.

Ne2H:
LvOL Group Norms Worksheet on page 23
Poster Board or Dry Erase Board
Markers

MSG:
Establish expectations and a foundation of trust for the group. In order for your group to be successful the first order of business is to establish group norms. This step is essential to group cohesion and ownership.

© 2009 Allyson Bowen, LISW-CP

Inclusion: We all Belong

 CTA:
Educate the girls of the importance of group norms. If they are not familiar with the term "norm" give them the definition. A norm is an expectation of appropriate behavior within a group. It can also be defined as the rules for a group. Help them understand the importance of knowing what is expected within the context of a group to be more successful. Allow the girls to brain storm out loud possible group norms and have someone write them on the poster board or dry erase board. After they are finished brain storming decide on the final norms for the group. Once a set of norms have been agreed upon have the girls complete the Group Norms Worksheet by listing the norms in the space provided and at the end have each girl pass their sheet around for the other girls to sign accepting the "terms of the agreement" for their group.

Two important points to consider. First, to insure group cohesion and trust, make sure there is emphasis on confidentiality, being a good listener, respecting others view point and making a conscious effort not to be relationally aggressive. Second, decide if there will there be a consequence for breaking a rule and should the girls have a say as to the consequence. Have a discussion.

 LvOL:
We all belong in the sisterhood, living, learning and loving ourselves and each other!

© 2009 Allyson Bowen, LISW-CP

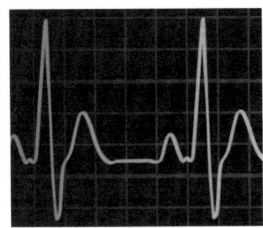

Conversation Card

Find out something about someone that starts with one of the letters.

For Example:
V Susan plays the violin
B Lealia's favorite candy is Butterfinger.
S Mandy is on the swim team

T _____

K _____

L _____

N _____

H _____

A _____

M _____

E _____

D _____

J _____

H _____

R _____

P _____

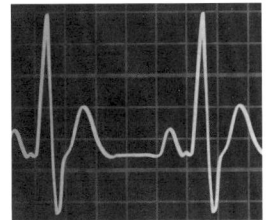

Livin' Out Loud Group Norms
WORKSHEET

1. _____
2. _____
3. _____
4. _____
5. _____

We agree to abide by the norms set forth in our Livin' Out Loud group.

_____ _____

_____ _____

_____ _____

_____ _____

_____ _____

_____ _____

_____ _____

© 2009 Allyson Bowen, LISW-CP

"Current Mood"

WU:
Opening Activity: "Emotion Commotion"

Photocopy the "Emotion Commotion" words and cut them into strips. Fold and place them in a hat or bowl. As the girls arrive have them draw a word. They are to begin to act out this emotion and continue until time is called. Call the girls to a circle and have them try to guess what emotion each girl was portraying. Notice some of the more simple emotion words the girls may use. This will be a good spring board activity into this week's lesson where emotions will be explored.

Ne2H:
Scissors
Plastic baggie for each girl
Colored paper
Hat or Bowl
"Emotion Commotion" words page 27
Copy of Emoticons on pages 28-30
Copy of Mood Cards page 31

Before the girls arrive photocopy a set of emoticons for each girl. For fun photocopy them on colored paper. Also, photocopy the mood cards. You may want to photocopy several pages as each girl will use a mood card at the beginning of every session.

MSG:
Identify emotions and learn how our feelings impact thoughts, reactions and interactions with others.

"Current Mood"

 CTA:

Have the girls cut out the emoticons and place them in the plastic baggie.

While they are cutting out the emoticons have an open discussion about emotions. Ask how they would define some of the emotions. For example, discuss the emotion perplexed. What does perplexed mean? Have they ever experienced feeling perplexed? Ask if there are others they may not know how to define.

Discuss the power of emotions. They can dictate how we feel about a person or situation. They can protect us when we trust them. For example, if we experience fear it could be a warning sign to continue with caution in a situation.

Now, have them choose one emoticon that represents their "current mood." Ask several of the girls to share why they chose a particular emotion. Give each of them a mood card to complete.

Directions for the Mood Card:

- Have them fill in the blank with the emotion word the emoticon represents. Then complete the rest of the card.

- Give them a few minutes to complete silently.

Discuss the following.

- Do you feel your mood affects the way you interact with others?

- Do you feel you have control over your moods/emotions?

- Do you use emoticons to represent your mood on the internet?

 # "Current Mood"

The trend for many blogs, posts or social networking sites is to list your "current mood." Using emoticons or smileys you can identify your emotions. By learning to identify emotions we become more self aware. When we are more aware we feel more in control and can make better decisions. With this new found awareness our self concept increases and we communicate more effectively and manage stress. Overall, becoming emotionally literate will enhance who we are as an individual and how we interact with others in the real world and in cyber world. Discuss with the girls this process and how to apply it in everyday situations.

 ## LvOL:
Become in tune with your "Current Mood" and consider how it could effect your interactions with others.

*As noted in the opening section the "Current Mood" emoticons and Mood Card will be used at the start of every session. This will be a part of the "WU" section and should take about 10-15 minutes.

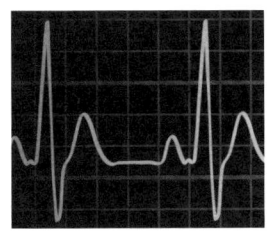

"Emotion Commotion" Words

SURPRISED	CURIOUS
HORRIFIED	JEALOUS
AGONIZING	BASHFUL
PROUD	MISCHIEVOUS
SYMPATHETIC	HYSTERICAL
FRUSTRATED	CONFIDENT
GRIEVING	LONELY
MISERABLE	ECSTATIC
EXCITED	VICTORIOUS
HAPPY	SHOCKED

© 2009 Allyson Bowen, LISW-CP

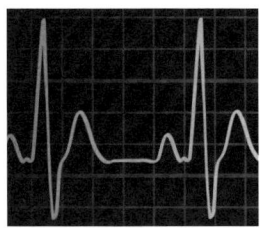

Emoticons

DEPRESSED	CONFUSED	BASHFUL
EMBARASSED	CONFIDENT	EXHAUSTED
TERRIFIED	SAD	LOVED
FURIOUS	MISERABLE	SLEEPY

© 2009 Allyson Bowen, LISW-CP

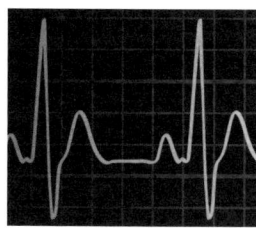

Emoticons

MUSICAL	 HAPPY	 SHY
 CHILDISH	 TIRED	 PLAYFUL
 GREEDY	 LONELY	 BORED
 FRUSTRATED	 ECSTATIC	 MISCHIEVOUS

© 2009 Allyson Bowen, LISW-CP

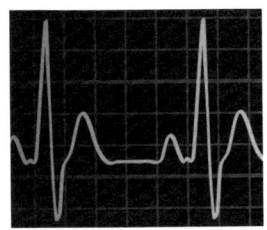

Emoticons

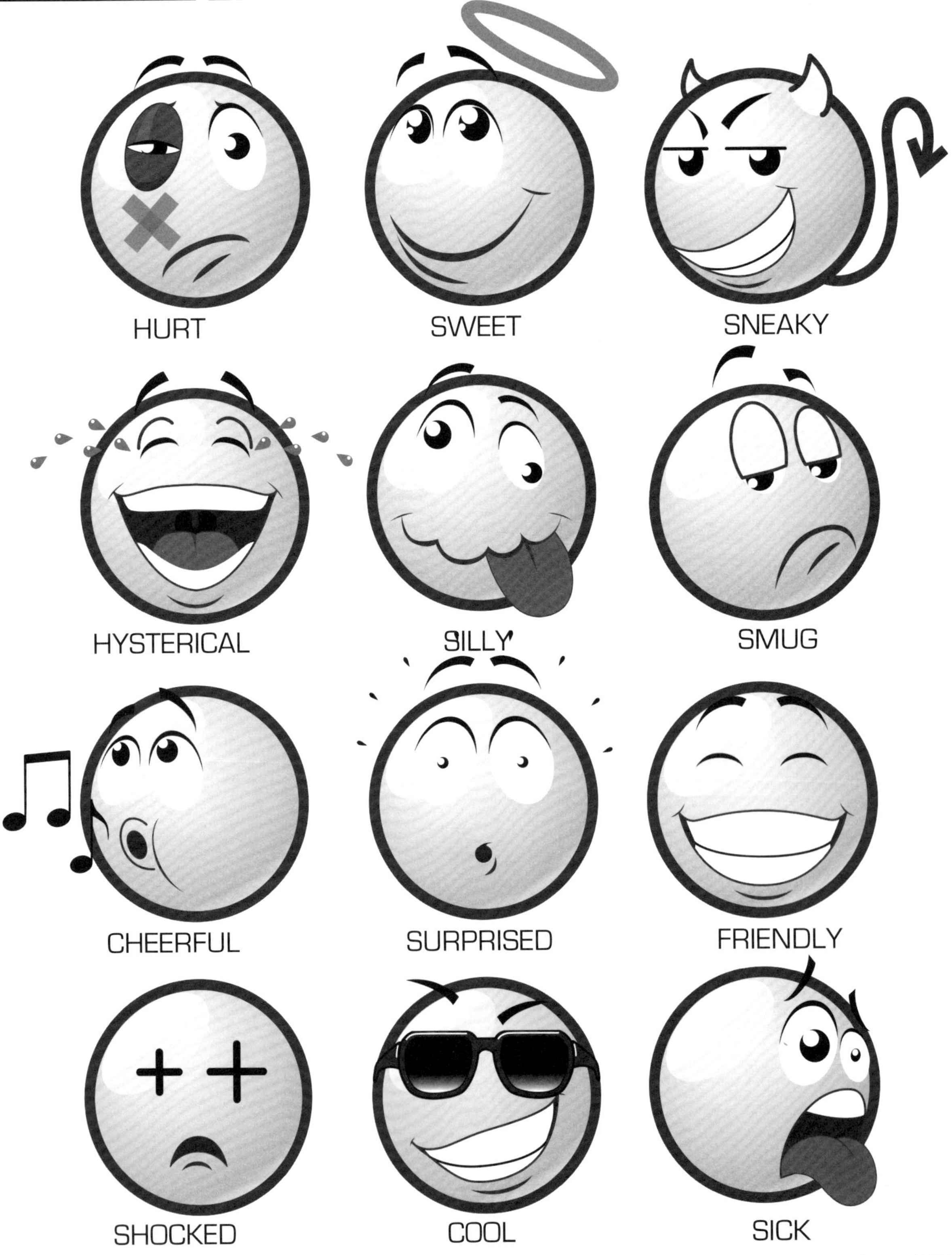

HURT	SWEET	SNEAKY
HYSTERICAL	SILLY	SMUG
CHEERFUL	SURPRISED	FRIENDLY
SHOCKED	COOL	SICK

© 2009 Allyson Bowen, LISW-CP

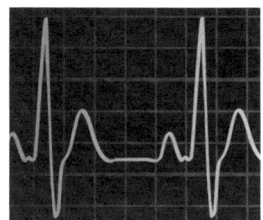

Mood Cards

My current mood is_____.

I feel_____ because_____
_____.

I like / do not like (circle one) how this mood/emotion makes me feel.

What can I do to maintain or change this emotion?
_____
_____
_____

My current mood is_____.

I feel_____ because_____
_____.

I like / do not like (circle one) how this mood/emotion makes me feel.

What can I do to maintain or change this emotion?
_____
_____
_____

© 2009 Allyson Bowen, LISW-CP

# Livin' Out Loud

 ## WU:
Current Mood and Mood Card

 ## Ne2H:
Livin' Out Loud (LvOL) Worksheet page 34

 ## MSG:
Explore individuality, define responsible living, identify characteristics and traits of Livin' Out Loud Responsibly

 ## CTA:
Have the girls complete the LvOL Worksheet. Discuss their responses. Do not allow them to sail by with surface answers such as "don't IM about someone behind their back." Challenge them to dig deep and realistically into to how they will prevent themselves from not IMing about others behind their back.

Discuss the following questions that apply to cyber world:

- Is a blog or post on a site such as "Live Journal" today's version of a diary?

- Do you feel posting information about yourself on a social networking site such as Facebook or MySpace, should be private from your parents or other adults as it would be in a diary?

- Do you feel you should have freedom of speech on the internet?

© 2009 Allyson Bowen, LISW-CP

Livin' Out Loud

Share the following:

- Did you know when you post information on the internet it can stay there forever! Even if you remove the information from your site if someone else copied, cut or pasted any information then it is still floating around cyber world.

Most of you were born into this world of technology and your uncanny ability to navigate cyber world is amazing. We admire your skills with technology such as the internet and cell phones but realize that somewhere along the way there was a disconnect in educating you on the appropriateness of not only using technology but also engaging others while using it. It is a social life line for many and we do not want to unplug you from that connection but our goal is to help you stay connected in a more responsible and respectable way.

The next few lessons will focus on becoming more cyber savvy.

 ## LvOL:
You came into this world to live out loud, now live it responsibly in the real world and cyber world!

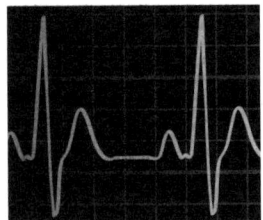

Livin' Out Loud
W O R K S H E E T

1. What does "Livin' Out Loud" mean to you?
   _____
   _____

2. Do you think Livin' Out Loud is positive, negative or both?
   _____
   _____

3. Do you feel you live out loud?   ☐ Yes   ☐ No
   Explain your answer.
   _____
   _____

4. List three ways you can live out loud positively and responsibly.
   _____
   _____

5. List three ways you can live out loud responsibly with technology (i.e. internet, mobile phone).
   _____
   _____

© 2009 Allyson Bowen, LISW-CP

# Face it: Fiction, Fear, Fact?

 WU:
Current Mood and Mood Card

 Ne2H:
Perception Picture page 37
Who do you know? Worksheet page 38
What do you know? Worksheet page 39

 MSG:
The goal is for them to get to know each other better in order for them to feel comfortable learning alongside each other and challenging perceptions of others.

 CTA:
Have the girls view the perception picture. Ask them if they see two faces or a fancy glass. Solicit first reactions. Some of the girls will see one or the other image and some will see both. Ask who is correct, the ones who see the faces or the fancy glass. The answer is, they are both correct. However the point is that our perception is our reality but it may not be the reality.

Give the girls the Who Do You Know? worksheet and have them complete and pass back to you. Once everyone has completed the worksheet pass out the What Do You Know? worksheet. Give the girls the opportunity to spread out and have their own space while working on the activity. Have them work silently. While they are working on the activity review the Who Do You Know? worksheets and pair them with the person they listed as knowing least. This could get tricky but do your best to pair girls based on who they know the least or listed in the bottom few of who they stated they know least.

After the worksheets are finished call out the pairs and tell them to go together to a spot in the room. Once in their spot they are to spend time talking, asking

© 2009 Allyson Bowen, LISW-CP

35

# Face it: Fiction, Fear, Fact?

questions and generally getting to know each other. They may want to discuss what they thought they knew about this person and ask if it is true. They must talk the entire time designated for this part of the activity. If you notice any two girls struggling, intervene and suggest questions they can ask each other. For example, what's the last song you downloaded on your i-pod? What's your favorite movie? What's your favorite color?

After the interview time
bring the girls back together and discuss the following:

Reflecting over your original writing, is this person who you really thought they were? What did you learn? Were there any misconceptions? Were there any barriers or fears about this person? For example, you thought they were "stuck up" or "not nice"? Discuss how our fears at times can be a barrier in getting to know someone. Now that they have had time to pause and reflect, determine if what they knew was based on fiction, fear or fact and have each girl go around and share one unique or positive trait they learned about this person.

LvOL:
In your everyday interactions with others pause, reflect and decide if what you think you know about someone is based on Fiction, Fear or Fact.

© 2009 Allyson Bowen, LISW-CP

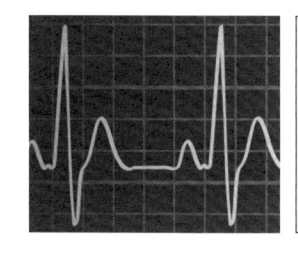

Perception Picture

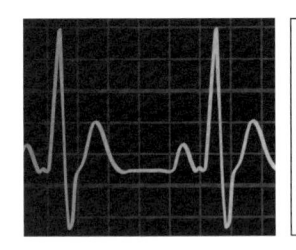

Who Do You Know?
WORKSHEET

Number your worksheet in numeric order based on the number of girls in the group. For example if you have 10 girls in the group number the card 1-10. List each girls name in your group based on who you know best to who you know least with 1 (one) being who you know best. When you have completed the worksheet turn in to the leader.

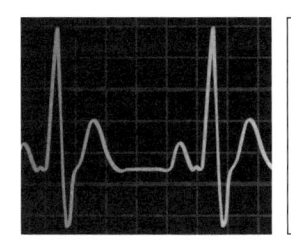

What Do You know?
WORKSHEET

Considering the list you just made on the Who Do You Know Worksheet, write one thing you think you know about each girl. If you need more room write on the back.

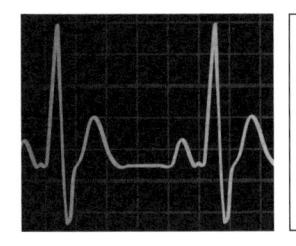

What Do You know?
WORKSHEET

© 2009 Allyson Bowen, LISW-CP

Cyber World

WU:
Current Mood and Mood Card

Ne2H:
Cyber Survey pages 44-45
Dry Erase Board or flip chart

MSG:
Evaluate technology usage
Discuss methods used in technology
Explore strategies for responsible electronic usage
Define Cyber Bullying

CTA:
Have the girls complete the Cyber Survey and turn in to you. This will give you a general overview of how much time and what methods the girls use with technology.

List the following on the board or flip chart:

- Instant Messaging
- Text Messaging
- Websites
- Email
- Chat Rooms (such as MySpace or Facebook)

Ask the girls to rank from 1-5, with 1 being the most used method and five being the least used method, which method they think peers use to tease, bully or be aggressive towards other peers.

© 2009 Allyson Bowen, LISW-CP

Cyber World

Answers: (Hertz, 2008)

Instant Messaging 67%
Chat Rooms 25%
Email 25%
Websites 23%
Text Messaging 16%

Define for the girls Cyber Bullying. Cyber Bullying is bullying behavior between peers where an individual is aggressively targeted, there is an imbalance of power and the behavior is repeated using digital technology such as computers or mobile phones. Cyber bullying can take place through instant messaging, mobile phones, text messaging, blogs, web sites, chat rooms or e-mail (Aftab, 2006; Hertz & Ferdon, 2008; Kowalski et al., 2008).

What have they experienced or witnessed? Typically, text messaging and chat rooms will come up as methods they are aware of that peers use frequently to be electronically aggressive.

Ask:

- Why do you think electronic aggression has increased?

- Is it easier to say something to someone through IMing, texting, blogs or emails? Why?

- Have you ever felt you could say whatever you want on your MySpace or Facebook site?

- What about anonymity? Are you really anonymous? Do you think you can be found? Do you feel you can hide on the internet or behind technology?

- Have you ever IM'd or "friended" someone that you did not know in the real world? There may be hesitation of disclosure. Continue discussion

Cyber World

Tips to Share:

- "If I know you F2F* then we can chat in cyber space!" (*F2F =face to face) Protect yourself from possible impostors. Do not trust someone who you cannot see. Remember friendships are built on trust and honesty; it is not a friendship if you do not really know the real person.

- Note: Gaming using Avatars, icons that represent an individual in cyber space, will be discussed in another activity. Gaming is different than communicating with someone who portrays themselves as a "real" person.

- If you can't say it F2F don't say it in cyber space! Don't post anything Grandma wouldn't be proud of.

- Would you be willing to attach a copy of your text messages, instant messages or social networking site to your college application or a job application?

- Be aware of "chatattitude"! Even though you cannot see someone while communicating with them remember to keep a polite and cordial tone. Cyber talk has become very savvy and your attitude can be relayed even in cyber space.

- They can find you! Just because you are in the privacy of your own home emails, IM's, and other forms of electronic communication are traceable. Many forms of electronic aggression are considered crimes.

- Consider making a copy of the tips for the girls to keep.

LvOL:
You are responsible for your electronic use! Be accountable for every "click" or "send"!

© 2009 Allyson Bowen, LISW-CP

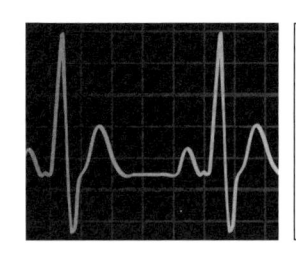

CYBER SURVEY

Check which answers apply.

1. How much time per day do you spend on the internet?
   - ❏ Less than 1 hour
   - ❏ 1-3 hours
   - ❏ 4-5 hours
   - ❏ 5+ hours

2. Do you have a social networking page (MySpace, Facebook, Friendster, Xanga, Bebo, etc)?
   - ❏ Yes, I have a page on _____ (which site).
     Go to question #3
   - ❏ No, go to question #4

3. What information do you have on your page? (check all that apply)
   - ❏ Name
   - ❏ Age
   - ❏ Hometown and/or state
   - ❏ Gender
   - ❏ School name
   - ❏ Orientation
   - ❏ Relationship status
   - ❏ Current city
   - ❏ Birthday
   - ❏ Pictures of you and your friends

4. Have you ever chatted with someone online that you did not know in person?
   - ❏ Yes
   - ❏ No

5. Do you think it is safe to chat with people online you do not know in person?
   - ❏ Yes
   - ❏ No

6. Do you IM (Instant Message)? ❏ Yes ❏ No

7. Do you text message (SMS)? ❏ Yes ❏ No

© 2009 Allyson Bowen, LISW-CP

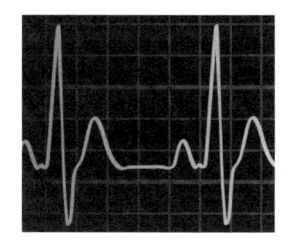

CYBER SURVEY

8. Where is the computer located in your home?
   - ❏ Living Room
   - ❏ Kitchen
   - ❏ Home office/playroom
   - ❏ My Bedroom
   - ❏ We do not have a computer in our home
   - ❏ Other:_____

9. Which method do you use most often to keep in touch with your friends? (rank in order of 1=most to least=6)
   - ❏ IM (Instant Message)
   - ❏ Chat Room (MySpace, Facebook, etc.)
   - ❏ Text Message
   - ❏ Email
   - ❏ Blog
   - ❏ Personal Website

10. What do you think is the definition of Cyber-Bullying?
    (check all that apply)
    - ❏ Using any technology to bully someone.
    - ❏ Same as face to face bullying except on the internet.
    - ❏ When an adult poses as a child and tries to lure the child to meet them face to face.
    - ❏ When a kid is tormented, threatened, harassed, humiliated, embarrassed or otherwise targeted by another kid using the Internet, interactive and digital technologies or mobile phones.
    - ❏ When electronic devices, such as cell phones or the internet are used to bully, tease or pick on someone.

© 2009 Allyson Bowen, LISW-CP

Cyber Technology CROSSWORD

👆 WU:
Current Mood and Mood Card

👆 Ne2H:
Cyber Crossword Puzzle pages 47-48.

👆 MSG:
Evaluate understanding of internet technology terms, create discussion about electronic usage.

👆 CTA:
Complete the cyber crossword puzzle. You may want to do a "pre-puzzle test" and a "post-puzzle test" to see how much the girls may really know. Discuss the formal terms and definitions found on pages 49-52.

👆 LvOL:
Use your new found "techno" knowledge to be an internet savvy citizen.

Crossword Answer Key:

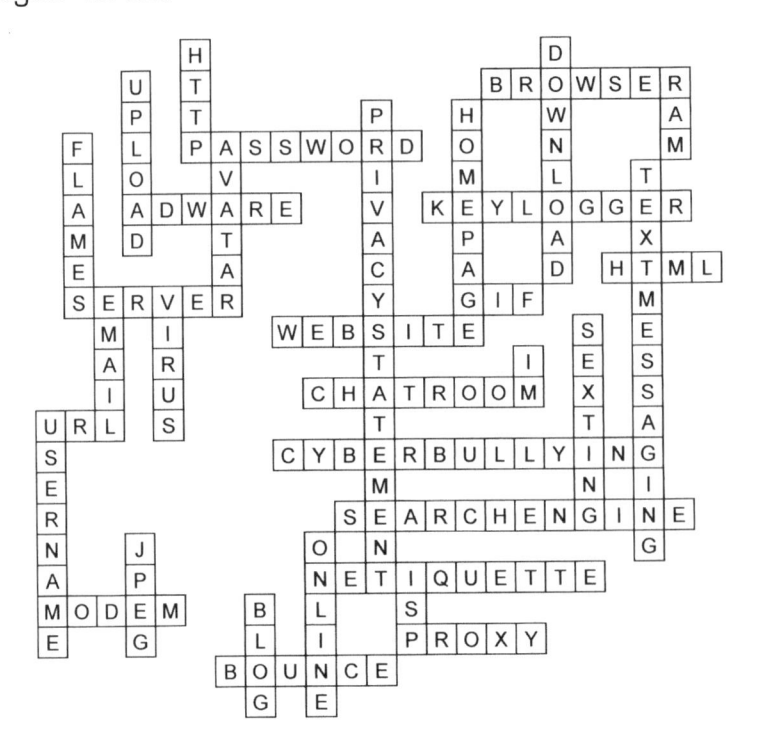

46

© 2009 Allyson Bowen, LISW-CP

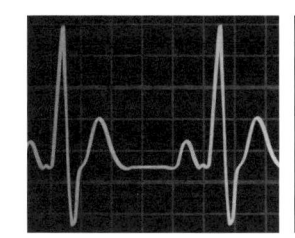

Cyber Technology CROSSWORD

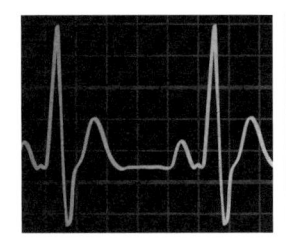

Cyber Technology Crossword

ACROSS

4. A software application used to locate and display web pages. The two most popular are Internet Explorer and Firefox.

9. A secret series of characters that enables a user to access a file, computer, or program.

12. Advertising software

13. Software that records all keystrokes typed on a computer.

14. 4 letters; Short for HyperText Markup Language the authoring language used to create documents on the World Wide Web.

15. A computer or device on a network that manages network resources; also takes your order at a restaurant.

18. 3 letters; Abbreviation for the global address of documents and other resources on the World Wide Web.

19. A site on the World Wide Web; many times ends with .com.

22. 2 words; A virtual room for conversation.

23. 3 letters; Abbreviation for the global address of documents and other resources on the World Wide Web.

24. 2 words; Teasing, harassment on the internet.

25. 2 words; A program that searches documents for specified keywords and returns a list of the documents where the keywords were found.

28. Good manners or accepted behavior on the internet.

30. Short for modulator-demodulator.

32. Server that sites between a client application, such as a web browser and a real server; acts on behalf of another.

33. E-mail that never arrives in the recipient's inbox; you can do this with a ball.

DOWN

1. 4 letter acronym for HyperText Transfer Protocol.

2. Copying a file from an online service; you can do this with music.

3. To transmit data from a computer to a bulletin board service, mainframe or a network.

5. Acronym short for Random Access Memory.

6. 2 words; Web document found on organization's Web site that details the type of personally identifiable information the company collects about its site visitors.

7. 2 words; First page you see on a site.

8. A searing e-mail or newsgroup message in which the writer attacks another participant.

10. An icon representing a person in cyber space.

11. 2 words; Messaging that takes place between two or more mobile devices.

16. Electronic messages over communications networks.

17. A program or piece of code that can corrupt your system; an infectious illness.

20. When a person takes a revealing or inappropriate picture of themselves and send as a text message.

21. 2 letters; A type of communication service that enables you to create a kind of private chat room with another individual in order to communicate in real time over the internet.

23. 2 words; Used to gain access to a computer.

26. 4 letters; Used as a photo acronym.

27. Turned on and connected to the internet.

29. 3 letters; Abbreviation for a company that provides access to the internet.

31. A publicly accessible personal journal for an individual; often reflects the personality of the author.

© 2009 Allyson Bowen, LISW-CP

Cyber Technology Crossword

👆 Definitions:

<u>Adware</u>: Any software that covertly gathers user information through the user's Internet connection without his or her knowledge, usually for advertising purposes.

<u>Avatar</u>: A virtual representation of the player in a game.

<u>Blog</u>: Short for Web log, a blog is a Web page that serves as a publicly accessible personal journal for an individual. Typically updated daily, blogs often reflects the personality of the author.

<u>Bounce (email bounced)</u>: a bounced e-mail is one that never arrives in the recipient's inbox and is sent back, or bounced back, to the sender with an error message that indicates to the sender that the e-mail was never successfully transmitted.

<u>Browser</u>: Short for Web browser, a software application used to locate and display Web pages. The two most popular browsers are Microsoft, Internet Explorer and Firefox.

<u>Chat Room</u>: A virtual room for conversation where a chat session takes place. Technically, a chat room is really a channel, but the term room is used to promote the chat metaphor.

<u>Cyberbullying</u>: Cyber bullying is bullying behavior between peers where an individual is aggressively targeted, there is an imbalance of power and the behavior is repeated using digital technology such as computers or mobile phones. Cyber bullying can take place through instant messaging, mobile phones, text messaging, blogs, web sites, chat rooms or email (Aftab, 2006; Hertz & Ferdon, 2008; Kowalski et al., 2008).

© 2009 Allyson Bowen, LISW-CP

Cyber Technology Crossword

Definitions:

Download: To copy data (usually an entire file) from a main source to a peripheral device. The term is often used to describe the process of copying a file from an online service or bulletin board service (BBS) to one's own computer. Downloading can also refer to copying a file from a network file server to a computer on the network.

Email: Short for electronic mail, the transmission of electronic messages over communications networks.

Flames: A searing e-mail or newsgroup message in which the writer attacks another participant in overly harsh, and often personal, terms. Flames are an unfortunate, but inevitable, element of unmoderated conferences.

GIF: Pronounced jiff or giff (hard g) stands for short for graphics interchange format.

Home Page: first page you see on a site the first document users see when they enter the site.

HTTP: Short for HyperText Transfer Protocol, the underlying protocol used by the World Wide Web. HTTP defines how messages are formatted and transmitted, and what actions Web servers and browsers should take in response to various commands. For example, when you enter a URL in your browser, this actually sends an HTTP command to the Web server directing it to fetch and transmit the requested Web page.

HTML: Short for HyperText Markup Language, the authoring language used to create documents on the World Wide Web.

IM: Short for instant message, a type of communications service that enables you to create a kind of private chat room with another individual in order to communicate in real time over the Internet,

Cyber Technology Crossword

Definitions:

ISP: Short for Internet Service Provider.

JPEG: Short for Joint Photographic Experts Group.

Keylogger: Software that records all keystrokes typed on a computer.

Modem: Short for modulator-demodulator. A modem is a device or program that enables a computer to transmit data over, for example, telephone or cable lines. Computer information is stored digitally, whereas information transmitted over telephone lines is transmitted in the form of analog waves. A modem converts between these two forms.

Netiquette: Contraction of Internet etiquette, the etiquette guidelines for posting messages to online services, and particularly Internet newsgroups. Netiquette covers not only rules to maintain civility in discussions (i.e., avoiding flames), but also special guidelines unique to the electronic nature of forum messages.

Online: Turned on and connected to the internet.

Password: A secret series of characters that enables a user to access a file, computer, or program.

Privacy Statement: A Web document found on a company or organization's Web site that details the type of personally identifiable information the company collects about its site visitors, how the information is used — including who it may be shared with — and how users can control the information that is gathered.

Proxy: A server that sits between a client application, such as a Web browser, and a real server.

Ram: Acronym for short for random access memory, a type of computer memory that can be accessed randomly.

© 2009 Allyson Bowen, LISW-CP

Cyber Technology Crossword

Definitions:

Search Engine: A program that searches documents for specified keywords and returns a list of the documents where the keywords were found.

Server: A computer or device on a network that manages network resources.

Sexting: When a person takes a revealing, inappropriate sexual picture of themselves and sends it as a text message attachment.

Text Messaging: Sending short text messages to a device such as a cellular phone, PDA or pager. Text messaging is used for messages that are no longer than a few hundred characters. The term is usually applied to messaging that takes place between two or more mobile devices.

Upload: To transmit data from a computer to a bulletin board service, mainframe, or network.

URL: Abbreviation of Uniform Resource Locator, the global address of documents and other resources on the World Wide Web.

User Name: A name used to gain access to a computer system.

Virus: A program or piece of code that is loaded onto your computer without your knowledge and runs against your wishes.

Website: A location on the World Wide Web.

A-Z Power Me!
WORD FIND

WU:
Current Mood and Mood Card

Ne2H:
A-Z Power Me! Word Find Puzzle pages 54-55

MSG:
Identify strengths and individual characteristics

CTA:
Complete the word find puzzle. Discuss the characteristics used and the meanings. Have the girls create a "Power Me" list by identifying as many words as possible that represent who they are using each letter of the alphabet. Be creative for some of the more difficult letters like 'X,' 'Y,' and 'Z.' Refer to the list of Qualities, Strengths and Characteristics in the Appendix for girls to choose from.

LvOL:
Keep your "Power Me" list close by and practice living out loud A-Z!

Word Find Answer Key:

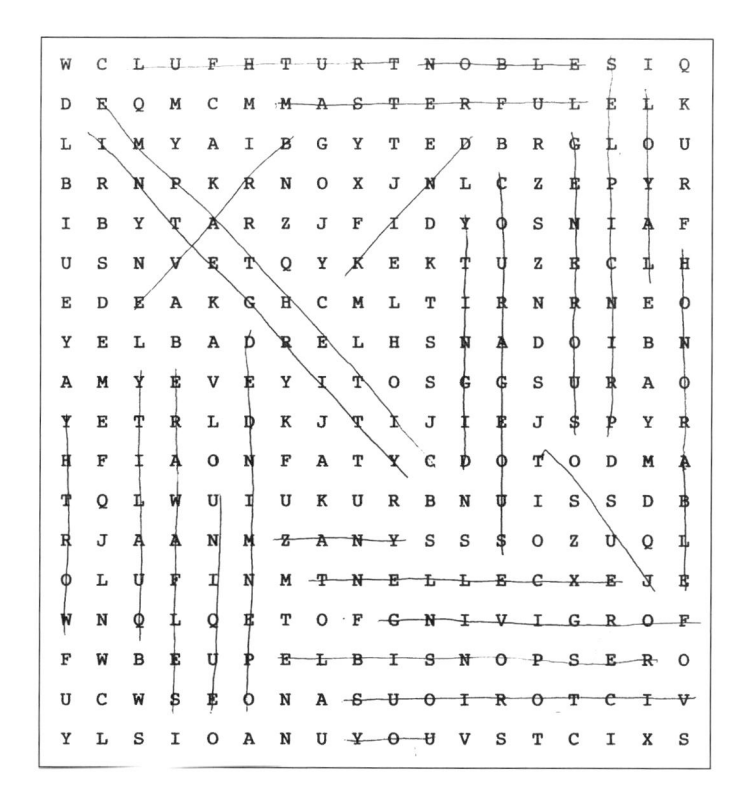

© 2009 Allyson Bowen, LISW-CP

53

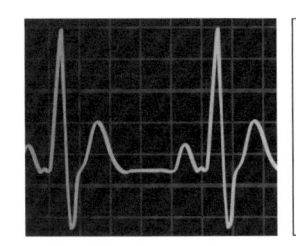

A-Z Power Me!
WORD FIND

```
W C L U F H T U R T N O B L E S I Q
D E Q M C M M A S T E R F U L E L K
L I M Y A I B G Y T E D B R G L O U
B R N P K R N O X J N L C Z E P Y R
I B Y T A R Z J F I D Y O S N I A F
U S N V E T Q Y K E K T U Z E C L H
E D E A K G H C M L T I R N R N E O
Y E L B A D R E L H S N A D O I B N
A M Y E V E Y I T O S G G S U R A O
Y E T R L D K J T I J I E J S P Y R
H F I A O N F A T Y C D O T O D M A
T Q L W U I U K U R B N U I S S D B
R J A A N M Z A N Y S S S O Z U Q L
O L U F I N M T N E L L E C X E J E
W N Q L Q E T O F G N I V I G R O F
F W B E U P E L B I S N O P S E R O
U C W S E O N A S U O I R O T C I V
Y L S I O A N U Y O U V S T C I X S
```

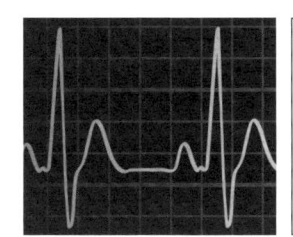

A-Z Power Me!
WORD FIND

WORD LIST:

able	integrity	responsible
brave	just	self aware
courageous	kind	truthful
dignity	loyal	unique
empathetic	masterful	victorious
excellent	noble	worthy
forgiving	open minded	you
generous	principles	zany
honorable	quality	

© 2009 Allyson Bowen, LISW-CP

55

The "I" Card

WU:
Current Mood and Mood Card

Ne2H:
The "Eye" Card page 58
Card Stock paper cut into approximately 6.5x3.5 size
Colored markers, pencils or paint
Scissors
Glue

MSG:
Diffuse the perception of anonymity while on the internet, you are never truly anonymous even in the privacy of your own home

CTA:
There is a misunderstanding among our youth today that they cannot get caught while on the internet in the privacy of their own home and while using a screen name.

Discuss anonymity with the girls. Ask, do you feel that if you use a screen name or code name that you cannot be found? Do you feel a sense of being hidden when you are behind the computer and no one can see you?

Give each girl a copy of the Eye Card. Have them decorate and then cut out the eyes. This may stir discussion about what they are going to do with the eyes. Once they are finished have them attach the eyes to the card stock paper.

Discuss how they are going to use the Eye Card. The Eye Card is designed to be placed on the front of your computer to remind you someone is always watching. In addition, you will have "I" statements to remind you of responsible internet use.

The "I" Card

Write the following "I" statements on your Eye Card. Laminate the Eye Cards if possible.

"I" Statements:

- I am responsible for my behavior on the internet
- I will STOP and think before I click
- I will consider others feelings before I send or post a message
- I will never give out my personal information
- I will not respond or engage in negative or mean behavior
- I will tell my parents or other adult if I receive a mean message or solicitation from someone I do not know

LvOL:

Put the Eye Card on your computer. Commit to the "I" statements every time you use your computer.

© 2009 Allyson Bowen, LISW-CP

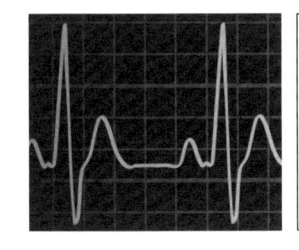

The "Eye" Card

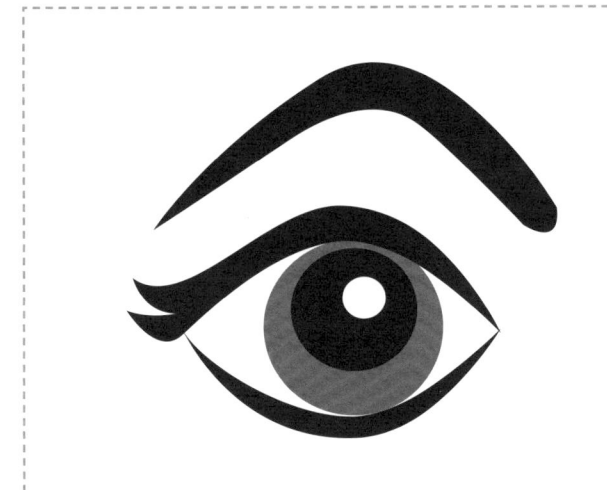

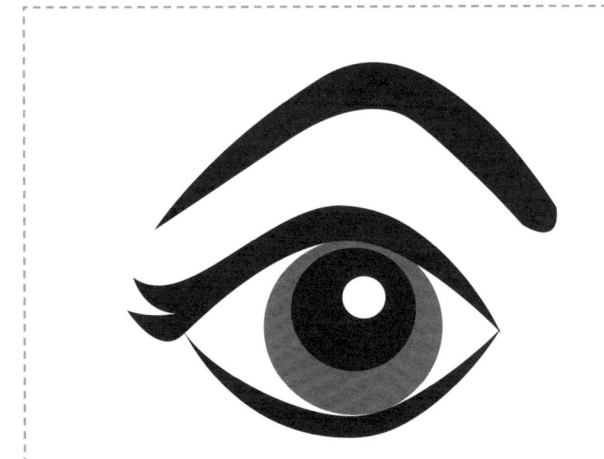

58

© 2009 Allyson Bowen, LISW-CP

"Avatar or Who You Are?"

WU:
Current Mood and Mood Card

Ne2H:
Avatar Mask Worksheet page 61

MSG:
Discuss the difference between real life representations of who we are to cyber world representations we create. Define characteristics of each representation that are positive and negative

CTA:
Avatars are object representations of individuals in cyber world many times used in online gaming. They can take on very life like personalities depending on the site where the Avatar is used. Avatars can be a cool way for girls to explore their personalities however it is important to investigate whether they feel it is a character they are playing or a perceived identity.

Ask the girls if they know what Avatars are? They may have used Avatars on websites such as Webkins or Neopets. Do any of the girls have an Avatar? What does she look like? What characteristics does your Avatar have that you also possess in the real world? What characteristics does your Avatar possess that you do not possess? Discuss how online personalities can sometimes be different from who we are in real life and while it may be fun to explore we must remember to be responsible when in character as an Avatar.

Tell the girls they are going to design and decorate an Avatar Mask. Observe how the masks are decorated. Then have the girls write a short description about their Avatar. What is her name? What is her "current mood"? What characteristics does she possess? (i.e helpful, caring, loving, friendly)

© 2009 Allyson Bowen, LISW-CP

"Avatar or Who You Are?"

Ask the girls if their personality and their Avatars personality are the same or different? Then have each girl list three characteristics that she possesses that are positive and characteristics that she could attribute to her online Avatar.

LvOL:
Check in daily with yourself to see if you are wearing a mask or practicing being authentically you!

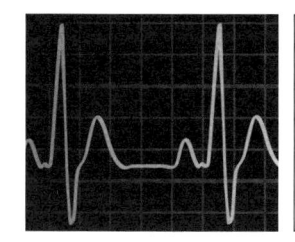

My Avatar Mask
WORKSHEET

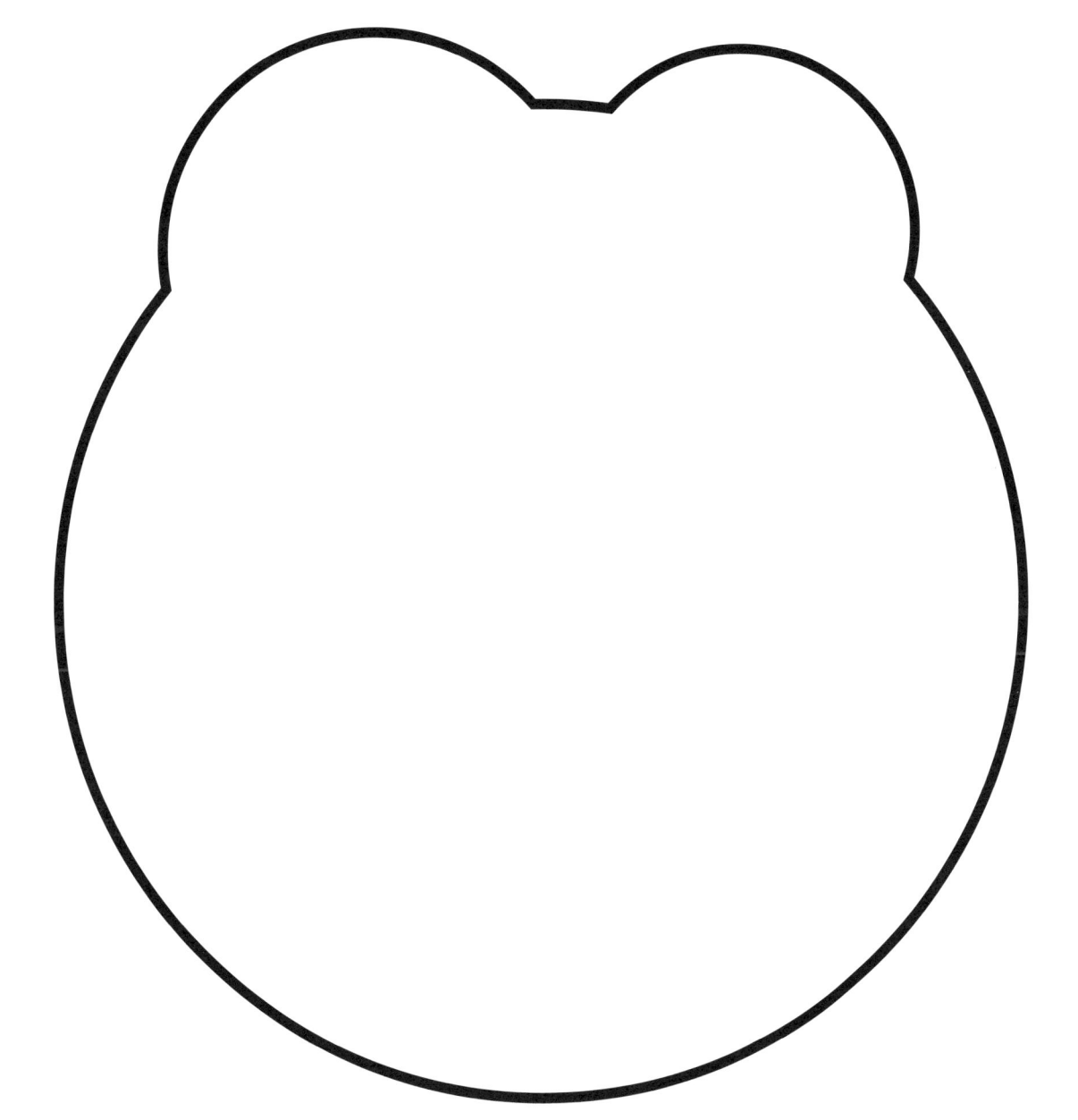

My Avatar's name: _____

Current mood: _____

Characteristics: _____

_____

© 2009 Allyson Bowen, LISW-CP

61

Me IRL (In Real Life)

WU:
Current Mood and Mood Card

Ne2H:
Me IRL Worksheet page 63

MSG:
Challenge the representation of self in cyber world versus real world. Identify qualities of self respect and confidence.

CTA:
Social networking sites have become a reflection of how girls view themselves. Many times a girl's site is more a character portrayal of who she thinks she needs to be than who she really is.

Ask who in the group has a social networking page such as MySpace, Facebook, Bebo, Friendster? The legal age to have a MySpace or Facebook page is 13 years old. How many of your parents have seen your page? How many of you feel your page is a real depiction of who you are?

Using the MeIRL worksheet have the girls create a profile. Encourage them to add their own unique style to the page to tell a story about themselves. Discuss how they designed their me IRL page and how it compares to their actual social networking page. Ask, which page more accurately reflects the authentic you? Encourage the girls to embrace becoming more authentic in how they portray themselves.

LvOL:
Be who you are! Be "Me IRL!" Practice daily using the characteristics and strengths from your Me IRL page.

© 2009 Allyson Bowen, LISW-CP

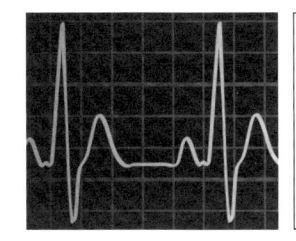

Me IRL (In Real Life) WORKSHEET

MY PAGE

Add/draw a picture

Dream Job or I aspire to be _____

My style or personality is _____

Friends say I am _____

I rock to _____ (Favorite music)

Yummy _____ (Favorite Food)

Fast Fact: (surprise us) _____

Hobbies _____

I can't live without _____

People say I'm _____

_____ annoys me

Favorite subject _____

I am good at _____

I know I am loved by _____

© 2009 Allyson Bowen, LISW-CP

63

Bullycide

WU:
Current Mood and Mood Card

Ne2H:
Bullycide in America Book*
www.bullycide.org
Research the internet for videos related to Bullycide
Dear...Letter Worksheet page 65

MSG:
Define Bullycide, discuss the impact bullying has on youth

CTA:
Give the girls the definition of Bullycide: suicide caused by bullying and depression (Marr & Field, 2001). Read several of the stories from the Bullycide in America book about youth who have committed suicide due to bullying.

Discuss the stories of the youth who took their lives due to bullying. Allow the girls time to process death by suicide if necessary. Have the girls write a letter to one of the victims of Bullycide or a letter of condolence to the victim's family. Explore with them what they would say, and what they feel they could do to prevent this from happening to another person.

Ask and explore the following. Do you know someone who is being picked on, teased, ignored? How could that person be suffering? Would you ever think that person could take their life? What can you do to step up and help?

LvOL:
Commit to step up and help someone who may be suffering. Identify who will help and the steps you will take to help them.

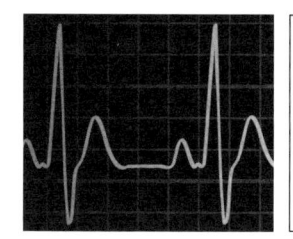

Bullycide Letter
WORKSHEET

Dear _____ ,

_____

_____

_____

_____

_____

_____

_____

_____

_____

_____

Sincerely,

_____

She is...

WU:
Current Mood and Mood Card

Ne2H:
She is...Cards on pages 69-71
Photocopy the cards onto card stock paper and cut out so that "She is" is on the front and the quality or characteristic is on the back.

MSG:
Identify characteristics of women who are role models and exemplify values, morals and attributes of an empowered lifestyle

CTA:
Are role models people we look up to and admire or are they people we envy and wish we could be like all the while never considering we could potentially possess the qualities they have. Open a discussion about role models. Ask, what is a role model? Consider their descriptions, people they list and how they perceive that person.

Identifying role models may not be something girls think of in detail. Many times, when role models are discussed, girls think of celebrities or athletes or possibly mom or dad. The challenge is to think beyond the person and examine the qualities of the person that could be emulated.

So let's play the She is... game. Take the She is... deck of cards and stack in the middle of your circle. Each girl will take a turn drawing a card. When they have drawn a card have them read the "She is" quality expressed on the card. After they read the quality on the card have them name a person they know that

She is...

embodies that quality. Have the girl share who that person is in their life if the other girls do not know her. Then they are to give 2-3 characteristics of the person named that represent the quality listed on the card. For example, if the girl names Aunt Elizabeth as someone they can trust, then two examples of why she trusts her would be she is a good listener and she always keeps my secrets.

LvOL:
Look up to your role model and recognize you can embody her same qualities. Practice implementing the qualities you listed about her.

STUDENT MONOLOGUES

Self Image

To look like others or be yourself? Which do you choose? I choose to be me because there is no other me or a person like me. Don't try to be someone else because in the end you will lose yourself on the inside or just be an empty shell. Self image…is it that important to look like someone else? I don't think so…love yourself, take care of yourself and just be yourself!

Laura – age 13

Fear

Too many people allow fear to take over their lives. They let it follow them…control them. They are afraid of challenges. But how will they know if they never try. Together we can fight fear. One day, fear will be afraid of us.

Shaily – age 12

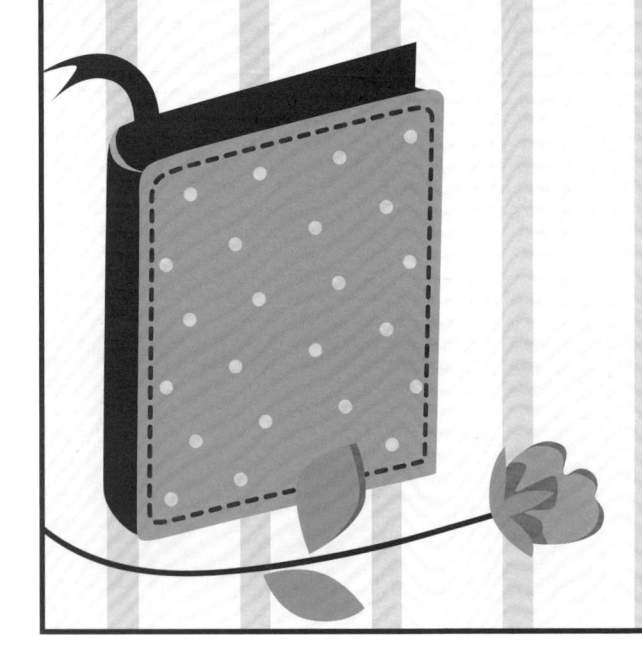

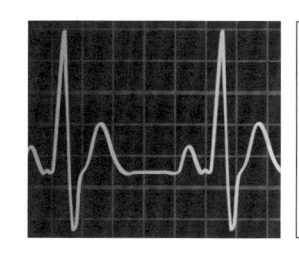

She is..... Cards

She is...	She is...
She is...	She is...
She is...	She is...

© 2009 Allyson Bowen, LISW-CP

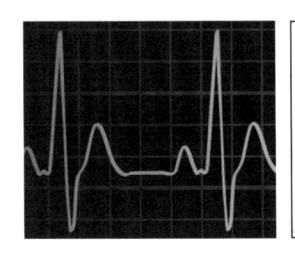

She is..... Cards

brave	someone who makes a difference
determined	someone with compassion
a leader	unique

© 2009 Allyson Bowen, LISW-CP

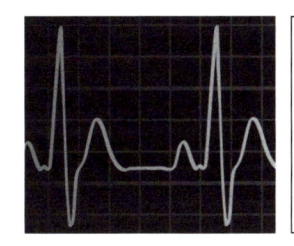

She is..... Cards

someone I am proud of	**someone I look up to**
someone I can trust	**someone I can talk to**
someone I admire	**a hero to me**

© 2009 Allyson Bowen, LISW-CP

Pieces of Me

WU:
Current Mood and Mood Card

Ne2H:
Pieces of Me Puzzle Worksheet* page 74
Plastic baggie
Colored markers, pencils, crayons
Plain paper
Scissors
Glue

MSG:
Identify strengths, qualities, individuality and demonstrate how these work together to empower one's self.

CTA:
Copy the Pieces of Me Puzzle worksheet on heavy card stock paper. Before they cut out the puzzle pieces have the girls mark the back of the puzzle so when the pieces are cut out they know which side is the front and which is the back. Once they have cut out all the pieces have them put the pieces in their baggie. One by one they are to take out a piece of the puzzle and decorate it with a quality, strength or character word (list in Appendix) or positive characteristic that represents themselves. They can print words, draw pictures or use any visual representation to describe themselves. Once all the pieces have been completed have the girls put the puzzle together. What a beautiful collage to depict their uniqueness and individuality. To keep the puzzle together, have them glue the pieces to the plain paper.

Pieces of Me

LvOL:

You were pieced together to be uniquely you! Use the Pieces of Me puzzle as a visual daily reminder of the strengths and gifts you have been given to contribute positively in your relationships and interactions with others.

*You can also visit http://www.b-muse.com/ATC-ARt-supplies.htm to purchase 4x4 puzzle blanks. They are approximately 50 cents apiece. The 4x4 puzzles are the puzzles used in the photo examples.

© 2009 Allyson Bowen, LISW-CP

73

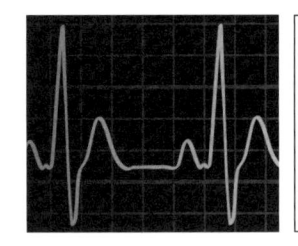

Pieces of Me Puzzle
WORKSHEET

74

© 2009 Allyson Bowen, LISW-CP

Pieces of Me Puzzle
SAMPLES

© 2009 Allyson Bowen, LISW-CP

75

Guess Who?

👆 WU:
Current Mood and Mood Card

👆 Ne2H:
Blank Star Card page 78
Guess Who Cards pages 79-92
Photocopy the cards and cut out before the girls arrive.

👆 MSG:
Identify strengths to deal with challenging circumstances and feelings.

👆 CTA:
One issue many girls struggle with is "I am the only one who has ever been targeted," or "I am the only one being picked on, teased or made fun of."

Have the girls close their eyes. Ask them to raise their hand if they have ever been talked about, picked on, teased, made fun of, gossiped about, felt alone, singled out, etc. (If they are honest, everyone should have their hand raised at this point.) Now ask them to keep their hand raised and open their eyes. Look around the circle. We have all been in the position of feeling like a target. However, it is a lonely, sad place and most of us do not like feeling targeted.

Now let's play the Guess Who Game. Ask the girls if they have ever looked at someone and thought that they have probably never been targeted, or would it surprise them if famous people they might admire have been targeted?

Explain the game. As you read the clues on the back of the card, they are to guess who the star is that you are describing. The girl with the most correct answers wins, if you want to have a winner. Don't forget to be prepared with a small token for the winner.

© 2009 Allyson Bowen, LISW-CP

Guess Who?

After you have completed the Guess Who Game, discuss how the different stars must have felt being targeted. Ask the girls what strengths they think the star used to overcome being targeted. Who do you think supported the star during their difficult time? Ask the girls to identify with one of the stars discussed and the strengths that helped that star overcome their situation. Use that as an example of what to do if they are in a challenging situation. Have them list the strengths the star might have used on one of the blank star cards. Encourage them to keep the star card with the list of strength words as a tool to use in a situation where they may feel targeted.

The purpose is not to compare our lives with theirs but to see that being targeted can happen to anyone. The difference in the outcome for anyone's life is one's ability to handle difficult situations.

LvOL:
You shine when you know who you are and love the star qualities within you!

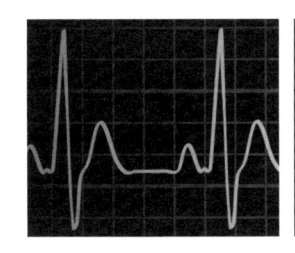

Star Cards

STAR CARD

© 2009 Allyson Bowen, LISW-CP

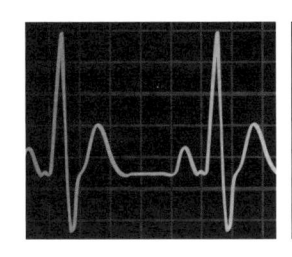

Guess Who? Cards

I was pushed around at school and did not fit in. I was threatened to get beat up after school. I turned out to be quite "Posh." I am one of the Spice Girls. Guess who?

VICTORIA BECKHAM

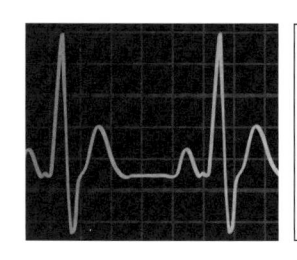

Guess Who? Cards

GUESS WHO?

Guess Who? Cards

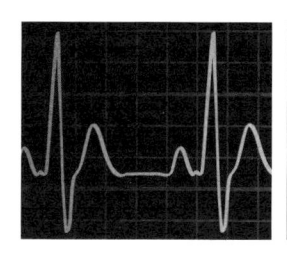

I was tall and skinny and felt like a freak at school. I was picked on and teased for my height. I have said: "If you're pretty but you're ugly on the inside, you're ugly on the outside too....gossiping, deceiving, taunting, and manipulating is very unfashionable."
Guess who?
TYRA BANKS

Guess Who? Cards

GUESS WHO?

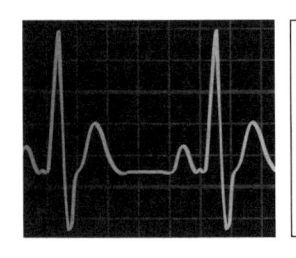

Guess Who? Cards

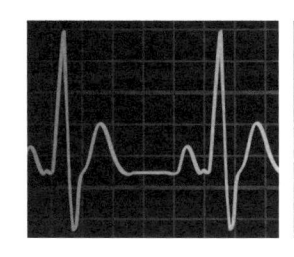

I was
shoved
into a locker.
I was taunted with "your Dad's a one hit wonder."
I have felt friendless, lonely and miserable.
I have the "best of both worlds"
and miles to go
Guess who?

MILEY CIRUS

© 2009 Allyson Bowen, LISW-CP

Guess Who? Cards

GUESS WHO?

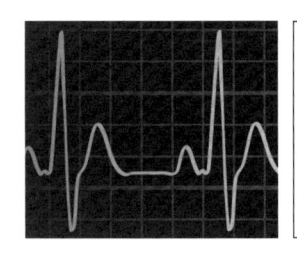

Guess Who? Cards

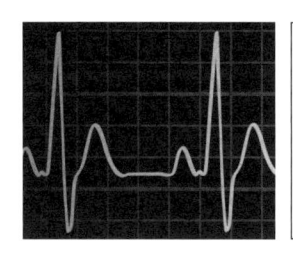

In elementary school I was ridiculed for my performance in a talent show. My families car tires were slashed. I was made fun of and bullied. I was in the Mickey Mouse Club.
Guess who?

CHRISTINA AGUILERA

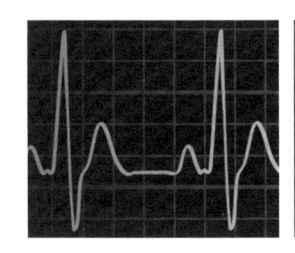

Guess Who? Cards

GUESS WHO?

Guess Who? Cards

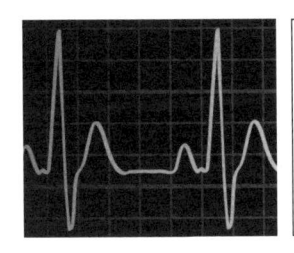

I was bullied for my weight. I had ugly comments written about me in permanent marker on a side walk. My families home was egged. I am currently a Dallas Cowboys fan
Guess who?

JESSICA SIMPSON

© 2009 Allyson Bowen, LISW-CP

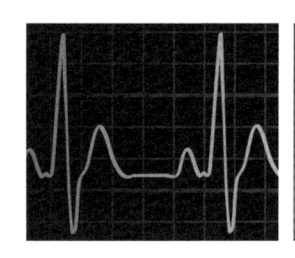

Guess Who? Cards

GUESS WHO?

88

© 2009 Allyson Bowen, LISW-CP

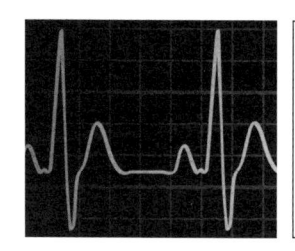

Guess Who? Cards

I was called an ugly duckling.
I was picked on for my black hair and dark skin.
I am known for being a house wife.
Guess who?

EVA LONG ORIA-PARKER

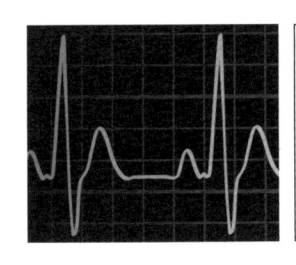

Guess Who? Cards

GUESS WHO?

Guess Who? Cards

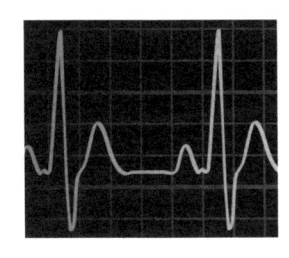

I was not a part of a popular clique. I was very self conscious. Kids in school would tease me, I was an outsider. I played a character on the T.V. show, The O.C. Guess who?

MISCHA BARTON

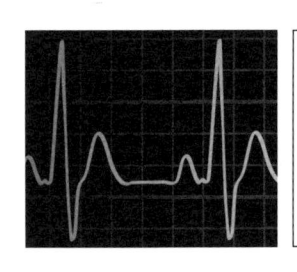

Guess Who? Cards

GUESS WHO?

© 2009 Allyson Bowen, LISW-CP

Mobile Me

WU:
Current Mood and Mood Card

Ne2H:
Mobile Me Worksheet page 95
Colored markers, pencils, crayons
Scissors
String

MSG:
Help girls to become more self aware of behaviors and actions.

CTA:
Girls are constantly on the go and do not think of what they are reflecting about themselves to others. Define for the girls the words character and integrity. Webster's Online Dictionary defines character as; a good reputation, the attributes or features that make up and distinguish an individual. Webster''s defines integrity as; adherence to a code of morals or artistic values. It has also been said that character and integrity are who you choose to be when no one is looking.

Ask the girls how they feel their character and integrity is reflected to others. Do they feel they have a good reputation or that they have features that distinguish them as an individual? Ask what they think people see when they look at them?

Have the girls complete the Mobile Me Worksheet by decorating the white area of the spiral with character words describing themselves. They can decorate the front and the back. Make sure they incorporate their name on the spiral. Once they are done decorating they can cut out the spiral following the black lines then

© 2009 Allyson Bowen, LISW-CP

Mobile Me

punch a hole in the center for the string. Thread the string through the hole and tie a knot on the underneath side. Hang the mobile. Watch it spin and reflect the many sides of your character.

LvOL:
Everywhere you go and everything you do let it reflect the genuine you!

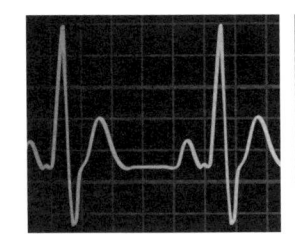

Mobile Me
WORKSHEET

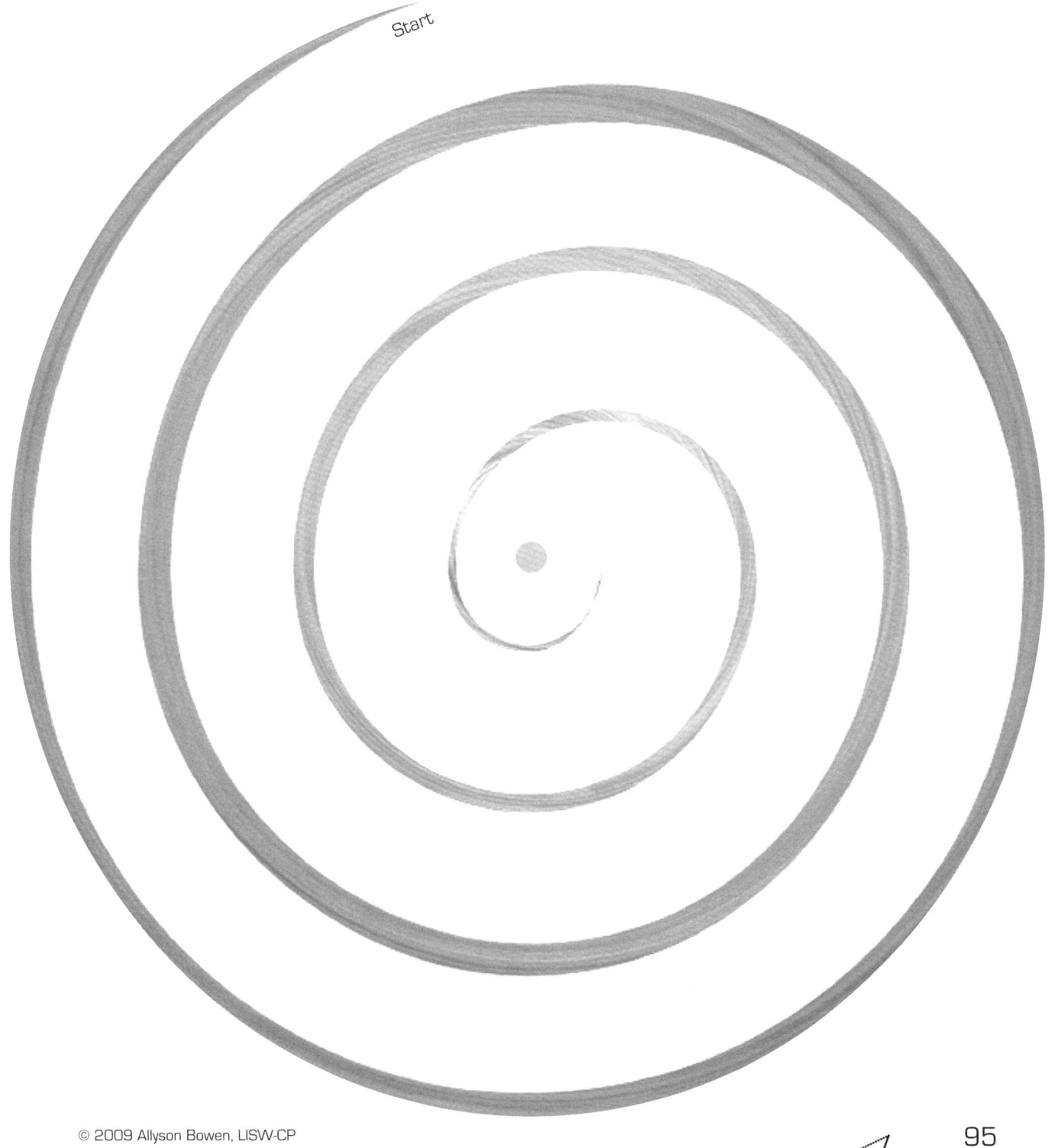

Start

© 2009 Allyson Bowen, LISW-CP

Circle of Influence

WU:
Current Mood and Mood Card

Ne2H:
Circle of Influence Worksheet page 98

MSG:
Challenge normative beliefs

CTA:
Open the discussion by asking the following questions.

- What do you believe in?

- Do you feel you have an established set of morals and values? You may need to define morals and values. Once there has been discussion ask the next set of questions.

- Do you believe it is okay to tease someone for the way the look? For example their ethnicity, or the way they choose to dress.

- Do you feel it is okay to laugh in class when someone gets the answer wrong or who doesn't read as well?

- Do you feel it is okay to leave someone out and not let them into your group or play?

The obvious answers to all these questions are "No," it is not okay. However, the reality is that it happens every day. Discuss with the group why they feel it is not okay to do these things, yet we all do them. Do we follow the crowd?

Circle of Influence

Is it the cool thing to do to pick on someone who may seem less than we are? Is it so common we do not think before we do these things?

Many times girls do not have an established set of morals and values therefore making it easier to be influenced by the crowd or perpetrate with ease. Ask the girls to think about who they hang out with socially. Do they know what these people believe in? Discuss with the girls how we become like those we hang out with. It may not be intentional or obvious but it is true. Have they ever thought about those people being their "Circle of Influence?"

Have the girls complete the Circle of Influence worksheet. They are to list one person's name on each line around the circle and under the name they are to list one value or belief they feel each person has. For example, Laura, "believes in always being honest," or "believes in being a good citizen." After they have completed this section ask them to consider how these people have influenced them. Did anyone have trouble listing a value or belief for any person in their circle of influence?

Finally, under "Me" they are to list three values or morals in their belief system. These may be new found beliefs after this discussion. Are there any common beliefs shared between themselves and the people listed in their Circle of Influence? Is it possible that any of these people could negatively influence you? Discuss the importance of surrounding yourself with people who believe as you do and have the same values.

LvOL:

Walk daily in the truth of what you believe! Surround yourself with others who have the same morals and values as you!

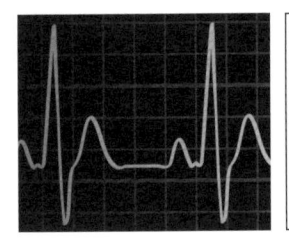

Circle of Influence
WORKSHEET

ME

© 2009 Allyson Bowen, LISW-CP

Hi-5

WU:
Current Mood and Mood Card

Ne2H:
Plain Paper
Tape or pins

MSG:
Girls will learn to give and receive praise, encourage girls to think of others and help them learn how to express they care.

CTA:
Have each girl trace one of their hands on a plain piece of paper. Then tape or pin the paper on the girl's back. Each girl is to go around the room and write one positive, encouraging word on each of the other girl's hand. For example, "compassionate." Encourage the girls to avoid superficial compliments such as "nice shirt."

It may help to review the Qualities, Strengths and Characteristics list in the appendix.

Once each girls "hand" is full of Hi-5's take the paper off of their back and give it to them. Then have the girls go around the circle and explain why they gave the praise or compliment to an individual girl.

Explore with the girls how it felt to give the praise or compliment. How did it feel to receive the praise or compliment? Discuss the power of giving words of

© 2009 Allyson Bowen, LISW-CP

Hi-5

encouragement to others. It's important we learn the skill of giving praise and encouragement, especially in the sisterhood. We need to support each other daily, celebrating others with the understanding that when we give we get so much in return.

LvOL:
When you celebrate others you celebrate the greatest gift within you!

Media Madness

👉 WU:
Current Mood and Mood Card

👉 Ne2H:
Movie/TV Show Review Card page 104
Media Madness

👉 MSG:
Girls will explore how media messages influence relationships and interactions with others.

👉 CTA:
Read the Movie and TV Show list included with the activity. Have the girls choose a movie or TV show and complete the Movie/TV Show Review card. Discuss briefly. This will give you brief insight and perspective to their views of certain media influences.

If possible choose a movie or TV show from the list and watch with the girls. If time is a factor, preview a clip from a movie or TV show or discuss a movie or TV show that most of the girls have seen. Some of the recommended movies/TV shows do have positive messages and offer good conversation. After you have chosen the show you will discuss use the discussion questions to create conversation about how the media influences our thinking and affects our relationships, especially our relationships within the sisterhood. All the questions may not apply to every movie or TV show.

Help the girls identify with reality and how confusing it can be when the media sends negative messages and calls it entertainment. Teach them to be media conscious and consider how the media influences how we treat each other.

👉 LvOL:
Do not be influenced by the mixed messages you receive from the media.

© 2009 Allyson Bowen, LISW-CP

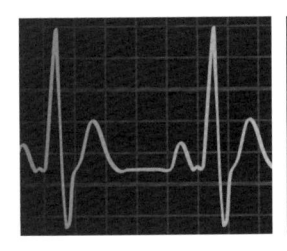

Media Madness

Movies
Mean girls
An American Girl Chrissa Stands Strong
The Clique
High School Musical
Odd Girl Out
Bring it On (all of them)
The Ant Bully
The Sisterhood of the Traveling Pants

TV Shows
Sonny with a Chance
i-Carly
The Hills
Gilmore Girls
Degrassi
90210
The Apprentice
The Bachelor
Desperate Housewives

Discussion Questions:

- Who are the characters?

- What role do they play? (i.e. mean girl, side kick, "wanna bees," target, etc...)

- Are the characters realistic?

- Who is your favorite character?

- Are there girls in your school like the characters in the movie or TV show?

- How are relationships among girls depicted?

- Are the relationships among your friends the same as depicted in the movie or TV show?

- Do the characters gossip, back stab, spread rumors, pick or tease?

- Do the characters make decisions based on the influence of others or do they make decisions based on what they believe as an individual?

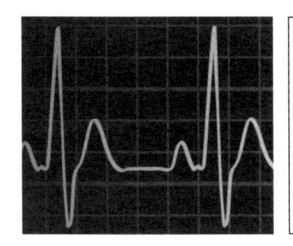

Media Madness

- What status symbols are portrayed? (clothes, cell phones, hand bags, etc...)

- Does the movie or TV show make you want more "stuff," as having "stuff" is what makes you more desirable as a friend or will make you more popular?

- How would you feel if you were in the "target's" shoes?

- Were there any solutions to the way characters treat each other or do they just perpetuate the problem by normalizing the behavior?

- How realistic are the solutions?

- Do you feel you could employ some of the tactics used to combat the way girls treat each other?

- Do you feel the "happy endings" are only for the movies?

- Do the strengths of the characters exist in the real world?

- What did you learn from this show?

- What role do the adults play in the show? Do they help or make the situation worse?

- Would you rewrite any of the endings? If so, describe your new ending.

© 2009 Allyson Bowen, LISW-CP

Media Madness
WORKSHEET

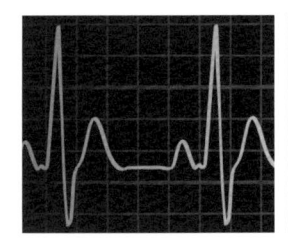

Movie/TV Show Review Card

1. What do you like about this movie or TV show?
   _____
   _____

2. What have you learned from this movie or TV show?
   _____
   _____

3. What are the positives of the movie or TV show?
   _____
   _____

4. What are the negatives of this movie or TV show?
   _____
   _____

5. Was anyone bullied in this movie or TV show?　☐ Yes　☐ No
   If yes, what happened?
   _____
   _____

6. Did the movie or TV show give you any solutions on how to handle friendship problems or bullies?　☐ Yes　☐ No
   If yes, what was the solution?
   _____
   _____

© 2009 Allyson Bowen, LISW-CP

Masterpiece

WU:
Current Mood and Mood Card

Ne2H:
Small Artist Canvas* or Card stock paper
Paint
Paint Brushes

MSG:
Identify unique qualities, individuality and how to express ones self.

CTA:
A masterpiece is an outstanding work of art. This activity is designed to help girls identify the outstanding individuals they were created to be. Art is one way to express or reflect who we are. Challenge the girls to think of an image, word or collection of items they feel reflect who they are. Have them to list these on a sheet of paper. Once they have done so ask them to consider how they would express this artistically.

Discuss with the girls that each of them is a masterpiece. How do they feel about being referred to as a masterpiece? Have they ever thought of themselves as an outstanding work of art? Explore how they were each uniquely created and there is no one else exactly like them. No two people have the same thumb print, not even twins.

Reviewing the list they created of images or words that reflect who they are, now have them begin to create their "masterpiece" on the canvas or paper provided. Remind

© 2009 Allyson Bowen, LISW-CP

Masterpiece

them this is not about artistic abilities, but an expression of themselves through art. When they have completed their masterpiece have them sign the art work and put their thumb print beside their signature to remind them there is no one else like them. They are truly a masterpiece!

Once the art work is completed place magnets on the back for attaching to the refrigerator or hot glue ribbon from the back to make a wall hanging.

LvOL:
You are a masterpiece! An outstanding, beautiful work of art!

*Inexpensive prepackaged artist canvas can be purchased in packages at an arts and crafts store or local discount mart.

Acting Up!

WU:
Current Mood and Mood Card

Ne2H:
Acting Up Cue Cards pages 108-113
Props you feel would enhance the role plays

MSG:
Practical interventions for addressing relationally aggressive behavior in the real world and cyber world through problem solving and role play.

CTA:
Split your group into two smaller groups (approximately 4-5 girls per group) have each group choose one of the Acting Up cards (depending on the age of the girls or grade level, you may want to choose which Acting Up cards they can select from).

Give the girls a few minutes to read over the scenarios. Next have the girls brainstorm the questions and possible responses to each scenario. Now have them role play how they would respond to the scenario. Encourage the girls to give as many details as possible. Challenge the girls to come up with realistic responses they feel would work in the real world or cyber world.

LvOL:
Practice solutions for coping with aggression in your daily interactions with others. "Act Up" to keep your interactions positive.

© 2009 Allyson Bowen, LISW-CP

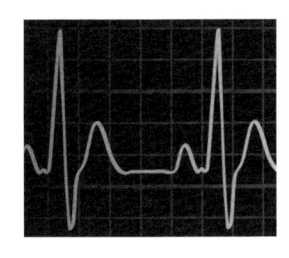

Acting Up Cue Cards

Kayla has been bullied at school for a number of years and has had a difficult time knowing what to do. She has been targeted for her weight and for her very different last name. The students have been very cruel. You are friends with Kayla and have witnessed the picking and teasing. Last night Kayla received a text message that said "you had better not show up at school tomorrow or else." She calls you to tell you what the text message says. How do you help her know what to do? This is considered cyber-bullying. What should Kayla do? Should she tell her parents or report this to the police?

Kim is from China. She tells her mom one day she wants blond hair and blue eyes. Her mom tries to explain that she is unique and special just the way she is. A few days later Kim comes home from school crying and informs her mom that several girls at school have been picking on her about her slanted eyes and that she just can't take it anymore. Is this relational aggression? (yes) What should Kim do? What should her mom do? How would you help Kim?

Acting Up Cue Cards

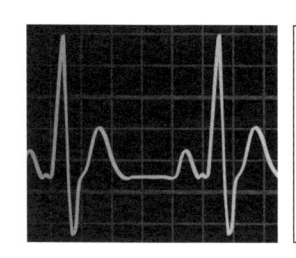

Several girls were instant messaging (IMing) one night. Maria is online and sees the girls IMing and joins the conversation. When she joins the conversation she asks why no one would sit with her at lunch today and at first no one responds to her. After a few inquiries, one of the girls finally sends a message that states everyone is tired of Maria thinking that she is so goody-goody and better than everyone just because she got the lead role in the school play. When Maria pleads her case and states she is sorry if anyone felt that way, the other girls send messages not accepting her apology and telling her she can no longer hang out with them. What should Maria do? Was there a better way the friends could have handled this with Maria? Should the girls have accepted Maria's apology?

Misty and Lauren are best friends. When they are together they get along great and have a wonderful time. Lately Lauren has felt left out when Misty is asked to go hang out with another group. Lauren is left standing there alone and feels excluded and humiliated as it is obvious she is not invited to hang out with the group. What should Lauren do? Is Misty being a good friend? Has anyone in the group ever been excluded? How does it feel to be excluded? What can you do ensure others feel included in your group? What it would look like to include someone in a group?

© 2009 Allyson Bowen, LISW-CP

Acting Up Cue Cards

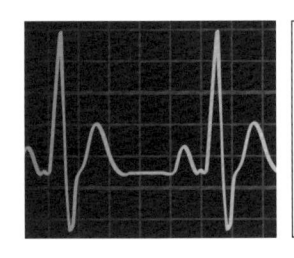

Nicole was teased for the clothes she would wear to school. Her clothes were cute and in style but just weren't from the popular stores where some of the other girls shopped. One day she walked past a group of girls who were snickering, laughing and pointing at her. What should Nicole do? What would you do if this were you? What would you say to the girls who were picking on Nicole? Is it right to pick on someone else for what they are wearing? Why do we pick on others?

Brianna reported that several girls in her class, whom she thought were her friends, had stolen her gym clothes. When she arrived home after school she received an instant message calling her a liar and a tattletale. She replied back feeling she needed to defend herself, "Well, you stole my clothes." Then the barrage started and she received over 30 instant messages full of put-downs, insults and name calling. Brianna goes to school the next day not knowing what to expect. The girls said nothing to her face to face. Why does it seem easier to say something about someone behind a computer screen? Why do you think anonymity gives people the feeling of power? What would you do if you were Brianna? What would you do if you were one of the girls who participated in the IMing? How should this situation be resolved?

© 2009 Allyson Bowen, LISW-CP

Acting Up Cue Cards

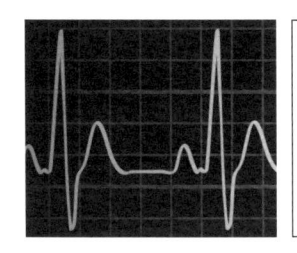

Ashley, Kelly, Ansley and Madison are known as the "fab four" and they think of themselves as being just that... fabulous! Ashley is the queen who rules the group and dictates how everyone should dress and creates her own rules as she goes to suit herself. If someone doesn't follow the rules they have to leave the group. Madison is fed up with Ashley and decides to do a three-way call with Kelly and Ansley. As the girls are talking and commiserating about Ashley they decide to devise a plan for the three of them to leave Ashley sitting in the canteen by herself tomorrow at school to prove a point that she cannot rule them any longer. After the call Kelly begins to feel bad for Ashley and calls her to give her a heads up about what is going to happen to her tomorrow and tells her everything Ansley and Madison said about her, but conveniently leaves out all that she contributed to the conversation. When Ansley and Madison find out what Kelly did how should they respond? What is a better way the girls could have handled this situation? If they are truly friends should they have sat down and discussed how they felt? If you know someone like Ashley do you feel they can change? What would be a positive outcome to this situation?

© 2009 Allyson Bowen, LISW-CP

Acting Up Cue Cards

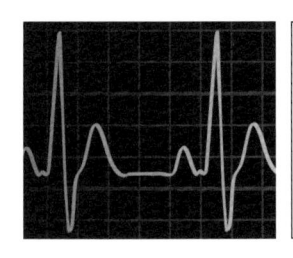

Candice receives an email suggesting she check out a new web link. When she clicks on the link it takes her to a web page that has been set up to bash her. There are humiliating comments, a rating of her and very provocative pictures that have been photo shopped using her face. Candice is humiliated and has no idea who would have done this to her. She cries silently not wanting her parents to hear her. When her dad walks by and sees her crying he inquires only to glance and see the computer screen with the web page displayed. Her dad becomes furious and begins to yell and put down her friends and threatens to call the police. Candice pleads with her dad not to do anything as it will only make it worse as she desperately wants to fit in at school. Candice goes to school the next day and feels very self conscious and embarrassed as she does not know who created the site or who is aware of the website. You and your friends are aware of the website and even know who created it. You can keep it to yourself, knowing it is wrong or you can report it. One of you wants to report it but the others do not. What do you do and why? You might get called a snitch if you report this do you take a chance? What tools can you use that you have learned that will empower you to step up and support Candice?

Acting Up Cue Cards

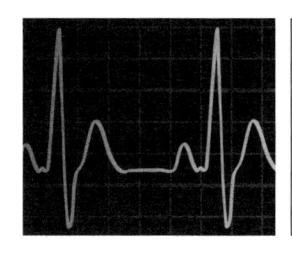

Tiffany is in high school and goes straight home after school to check her social networking page. She can't wait to see what messages she has received. She begins to read her messages and becomes horrified as she reads. The messages posted are "Tiffany is a whore," "Tiffany slept with three guys from THS", "Easy slut"! Tiffany is devastated and doesn't know what to do. Over the next few weeks the messages continue until Tiffany does not feel she can handle it any longer! Tiffany shares with you that she is contemplating ending her life. What would you do? Have you ever felt hopeless in a situation? Have you ever felt lonely and isolated and felt you had no one to turn to? As her friend what should you do?

© 2009 Allyson Bowen, LISW-CP

When Pretty in Pink turns Mean & Green!

WU:
Current Mood and Mood Card

Ne2H:
Pretty in Pink Worksheet page 116
Mean and Green Worksheet page 117

Photocopy the worksheets on corresponding colored paper if possible.

MSG:
Learn about jealousy and how to manage the emotion.

CTA:
Ask: What one word could represent these three words? Green, Mean, Envy. If the girls do not come up with the answer give them a second clue by asking the following question. Have you ever heard of the ugly green monster?

Answer, Jealousy! Define jealousy for younger girls. Explore why girls feel jealous of each other (insecurity). Ask them if they feel this will be something they can combat? How?

After you had a brief discussion, give the girls the Pretty in Pink and Mean and Green Worksheets. Discuss the words in the Mean and Green list and have the girls suggest other words that could be included. Have the girls list on the back of the Mean and Green worksheet what they might be jealous of in other girls.

Why is it so hard to celebrate another girl's gifts and talents? How do popularity and boys play into this behavior? Show the girls teen magazines or mention TV shows such as Desperate Housewives, The Hills or Degrassi (or other age relative show) and

When Pretty in Pink turns Mean & Green!

discuss how the media drives jealousy among girls. Discuss how jealousy fuels gossip and rumors in the real world and cyber world.

Now discuss the words on the Pretty in Pink worksheet and have them add words that could be included. One word that typically comes up is "nice." Many girls have been taught growing up to "be nice." Nice (just satisfactory) is overused and potentially sends the wrong message to our girls to be seen and not heard. The goal is for girls to be a voice, one of responsibility and empowerment, to stand up for who they are and not just be seen but heard as well.

After you have discussed the Pretty in Pink words have the girls list three actions to coincide with three of the words. For example, courageous, "I will stand up for what is right and not gossip about other girls."

LvOL:
Do not let jealousy creep up on you. Live "pretty in pink" powered by you!

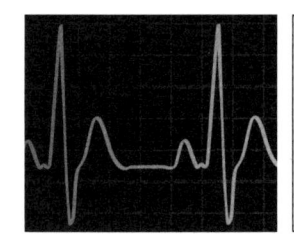

Pretty in Pink

Empowered
Confident
Savvy
Courageous
Determined
Skilled
Pep
Energy

_____

_____

_____

_____

_____

© 2009 Allyson Bowen, LISW-CP

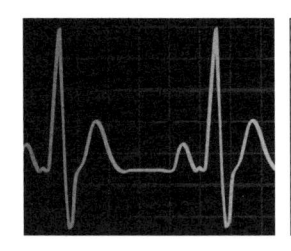

Mean and Green

Gossip
Exclusion
Jealousy
Envy
Rumors
Stares
Eye Rolling
Teasing

_____

_____

_____

_____

_____

Kindness Cures

WU:
Current Mood and Mood Card

Ne2H:
Kindness Cures Worksheet on page 121

MSG:
Explore opportunities to experience empathy.

CTA:
Empathy is the ability to understand and share the feelings of another (Merriam-Webster online) or to "walk in another's shoes." It's very difficult to just teach empathy. There must be opportunities to actually experience the emotion.

Too many times our girls feel powerless in having the resources or abilities to make a difference, but this will be their chance. For the girls to have a better understanding of empathy have them watch an episode of "Extreme Makeover: Home Edition" (check your local TV listing for time and station) with Ty Pennington. This is an "extreme" example of giving back due to man power and resources, but emphasize it's not the size of the task it's the size of the heart that makes the difference.

Challenge the girls to brainstorm and make a list of ways they can give back. They can give back to their school or their community. Remind them it is as much about giving time as it is talents. If possible, arrange with local agencies to have girls come and volunteer their time. For example, contact a local nursing home to see if the girls could come by and visit with the patients. Many nursing homes have patients who are lonely and would love to have someone talk with them, write letters, or read to them. If your girls are pet lovers contact a local pet shelter to see what the girls could do at the shelter with the animals.

© 2009 Allyson Bowen, LISW-CP

Kindness Cures

Help the girls create their own Kindness Cures event. Support them in the opportunity to fully engage in making a difference. Listed below are a few ideas to help get them thinking.

Ideas for making a difference:

Book Drive: Have the girls organize a book drive where gently used books are given and then donated to a local child abuse center or orphanage.

Change for Charity: Clean out your sofas, pockets and piggy banks for spare change. Donate the change to a local charity the girls feel passionate about or an agency with a mission that supports kids who are less fortunate.

Pennies for Pets: Have a penny drive and donate the money to a local pet shelter that rescues abused pets.

My Sister's Closet: Have the girls do a closet raid and encourage other girls and women to do the same. We all have clothes, jewelry and other accessories we no longer wear. Take the donations to a women's and children's shelter for those who may be in need of clothes.

Baby Shower: Throw a baby shower compete with baby decorations, games, snacks and baby gifts. The items received at the baby shower can be donated to a local pregnancy support agency.

Kindness Cures

Once they have decided on a mission, educate them about the group or organization for whom they will be volunteering or who will receive the proceeds. If appropriate allow them to meet the individuals of the organization.

Now it's time to organize the details of the event. Using the Kindness Cures worksheet, outline a plan for the event. Hopefully excitement has built and the girls are ready to accept the challenge of giving back.

After the event is over discuss how the girls felt being able to give back. Have them list 3 emotions they experienced while working on the event and seeing it through to fruition. What did they learn? Share with them any observations you noted as they planned the event and participated in giving back.

There is a list in the Appendix of National Organizations that allow teen volunteers or have suggestions of how you can partner with them to give back.

LvOL:
Give back daily. It doesn't have to be big, it starts with a simple hello, a smile or making someone feel special or welcome. Inspire!

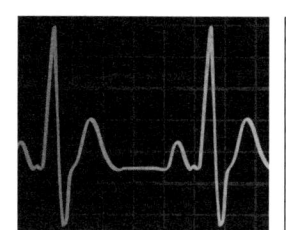

Kindness Cures
WORKSHEET

When will your event take place:

_____

Who will be the beneficiary of your Kindness:

_____

_____

What materials will you need to promote your event:
(i.e. posters, paint, flyers)

_____

_____

_____

List each group members name and their responsibility:
(i.e. Lisa, make the posters)

_____

_____

_____

_____

Healing the Hurt

WU:
Current Mood and Mood Card

Ne2H:
Healing the Hurt Letter page 124
Healed the Hurt Card page 125

MSG:
Explore forgiveness of past hurts, learn to heal hurts.

CTA:
Many girls are suffering silently due to past hurts that have never been resolved. They often think, "Well, I didn't need her for a friend anyway" to try and dismiss the pain or they may think, "She was the one who was wrong so she will have to come and apologize to me." This is part of the misconception of forgiveness and healing. It is not the perpetrator who is suffering. They possibly may feel they have done nothing wrong. This is a crucial point in helping girls learn to forgive. It is they who are suffering, not the person who hurt them. This acknowledgement is the first step in healing.

In addition, many feel they must speak directly to the one who hurt them and receive an apology in order for the hurt to be resolved. While this can be helpful, it's not a must for healing to occur. Forgiveness is more for the person who is hurting. A good analogy is to think of the person who is hurting being held in a cage. They are the only ones who hold the keys to freedom through their ability to forgive. However, they are unaware that they hold the key. Until forgiveness begins to take place, they remain in their cage of anger and hurt.

Another misconception is that if one chooses to forgive then they must also forget. This is untrue. We do not always forget a significant past hurt. However, there can be good in remembering once forgiveness has taken place. That may sound odd, but the reality is we do not have to remember the pain we can choose to remember the power of the release of forgiveness. We will emphasize that point later in the activity.

© 2009 Allyson Bowen, LISW-CP

Healing the Hurt

Forgiveness can be a complicated process and usually does not "just happen." Even when the steps to forgiveness have been laid out, it is realizing that it is the journey that is important.

Forgiveness for young people may feel somewhat subjective therefore it will require gentle intervention to help them reach a place of healing and forgiveness. Allow the girls time to understand forgiveness and then process the healing involved.

After there has been a time of understanding forgiveness have the girls write down past hurts that may still be lingering. Depending on the age group this could take some time. Help them understand this process is for any hurt they have experienced, big or small.

Once they have written out their hurts explore with them creative ways to begin to let go. For example, writing a letter to the person who has hurt them. This letter is not for the perpetrator, but a start at releasing all the emotions and pain associated with the hurt. This letter will have many edits before it is done. Once the final version is ready have them write it on the Healing the Hurts Letter worksheet. The next step will be left up to each individual girl and you can guide them on what options are best. They can keep the letter as a reminder of the process they went through to get to a place of healing, they can have a ceremony and tie the letter to a balloon and release it symbolizing letting go of the hurt, they can address it and put a stamp on it and ask someone to mail it for them, symbolizing they are "sending it away" (the person does not actually mail it).

After the letters are complete give the girls a copy of the Healing the Hurts Card and have the girls fill in the blanks once they feel they have released the pain associated with the hurt. This becomes the new "reminder" of the hurt. Encourage them to keep the card close by or with them at all times so anytime the thought of the incident occurs they can pull out their Healed Card as the new thought associated with the incident. The power of healing is in accepting that they have the keys to unlock themselves from the pain.

LvOL:
Live consciously in the power of forgiveness!

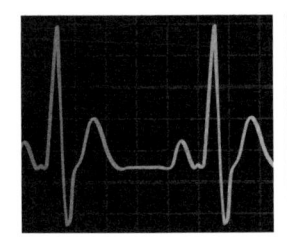

Healing the Hurt Letter

Dear _____ ,

Signed, Healed

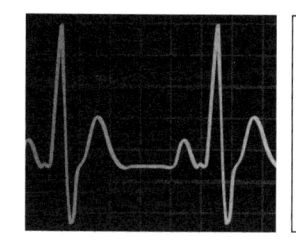

Healed the Hurt Card

On this day _____, and at this time _____ I choose to forgive _____ for the past hurts I have experienced. I will no longer allow this hurt to have power over me.

_____

Signed, Healed

On this day _____, and at this time _____ I choose to forgive _____ for the past hurts I have experienced. I will no longer allow this hurt to have power over me.

_____

Signed, Healed

© 2009 Allyson Bowen, LISW-CP

I Will Never...

WU:
Current Mood and Mood Card

Ne2H:
I Will Never Pledge page 127

MSG:
Never pass up an opportunity to do what's right and just.

CTA:
Review with the girls the I Will Never Pledge. Discuss the challenges they will face in keeping the pledge. How can they support each other to uphold the pledge? Review any of the activities completed within this group that have helped them to identify personal strengths that could empower them to uphold this pledge. Inquire about apprehensions they may have about the reality of committing to this pledge.

LvOL:
Live everyday with honor, respect, truth and love for yourself and others!
Never have regrets!

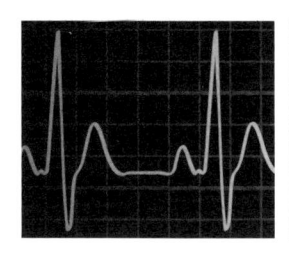

I Will Never Pledge...

Real World

I will never gossip or spread rumors about someone
I will never deliberately exclude or ostracize someone
I will never defame someone's name
I will never damage another persons property
I will never stand by and watch another person be targeted
I will never tease someone about their appearance or any other personal feature
I will never give inappropriate looks or other nonverbal gestures
I will never go against my character and pretend
to be someone I am not.

Cyber World

I will never post or give out personal information about
myself on the internet such as:
my name, address, telephone number
I will never post or give out the name of my school on the internet
I will never gossip or spread rumors about someone on the internet
I will never send a hateful text message about someone
I will never send inappropriate pictures of myself online or by MMS
I will never participate in online hostilities
I will never keep information to myself that should be reported to an adult such as cyber bullying: harassment, teasing, picking, threats
I will never meet someone in person that I only know through online communications such online games.

I agree to follow the "I Will Never" pledge.

© 2009 Allyson Bowen, LISW-CP

Ready for Business

👆 WU:
Current Mood and Mood Card

👆 Ne2H:
Ready for Business Worksheet pages 131-134
Colored markers, pencils

👆 MSG:
Identify themselves as worthy, respectable girls with a message of empowerment representing unique abilities and gifts

👆 CTA:
Photocopy several copies of the Ready for Business worksheet on card stock paper. Explore with the girls what they have learned about themselves over the last several weeks.

Define for them what the phrase "tag line" means. A tag line is a slogan or catch phrase. Brainstorm with the girls several tag lines they may have heard or ones they would create for someone they know. Now have the girls create their own tag line. Give them a little time to work on this part of the activity. Once they are finished have them choose one of the "business cards" from the Ready for Business worksheets. Have them cut out the "business card" and decorate it. After they have decorated the card have them add their name and their tag line. Now they have their own business card that represents their personality. When all the girls are done have the girls to begin to pass around their card and have each girl fill in a blank on the back of the card with one positive power word they feel represents the girl who's name is on the front. The girls are Ready for Business now!

Ready for Business

Encourage them to keep the card with them as a representation and a reminder of who they are.

If the girls want to trade cards with each other photocopy them on a color copier.

LvOL:

You have power, now you are ready for business! Walk daily in the acknowledgment of who you are, loving that person and possessing the ability to step out and shine! Go forth and do good! "be.love.do"

STUDENT MONOLOGUES

Be The Difference

There are many things in the world that people are unhappy about but they don't step up to change. They wait and wait and then complain when things don't change. Don't be those people. Step up to the change and don't hold back. Be the person that makes a difference. Be the person that makes the change.

        Taylor – age 13

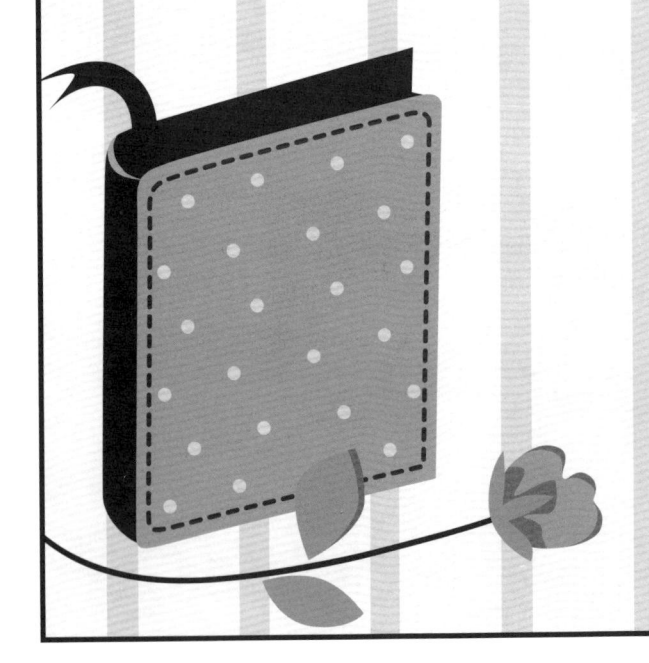

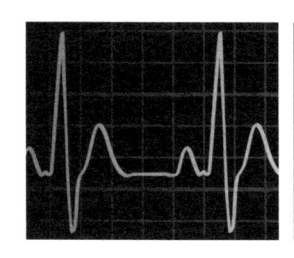

Ready for Business

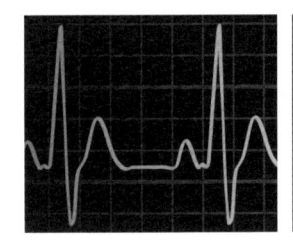

Ready for Business

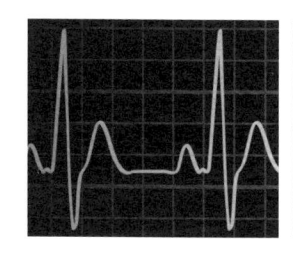

Ready for Business

© 2009 Allyson Bowen, LISW-CP

133

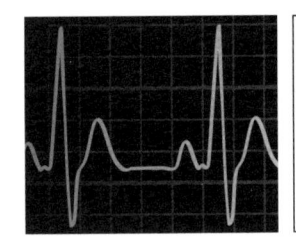

Ready for Business

Appendix

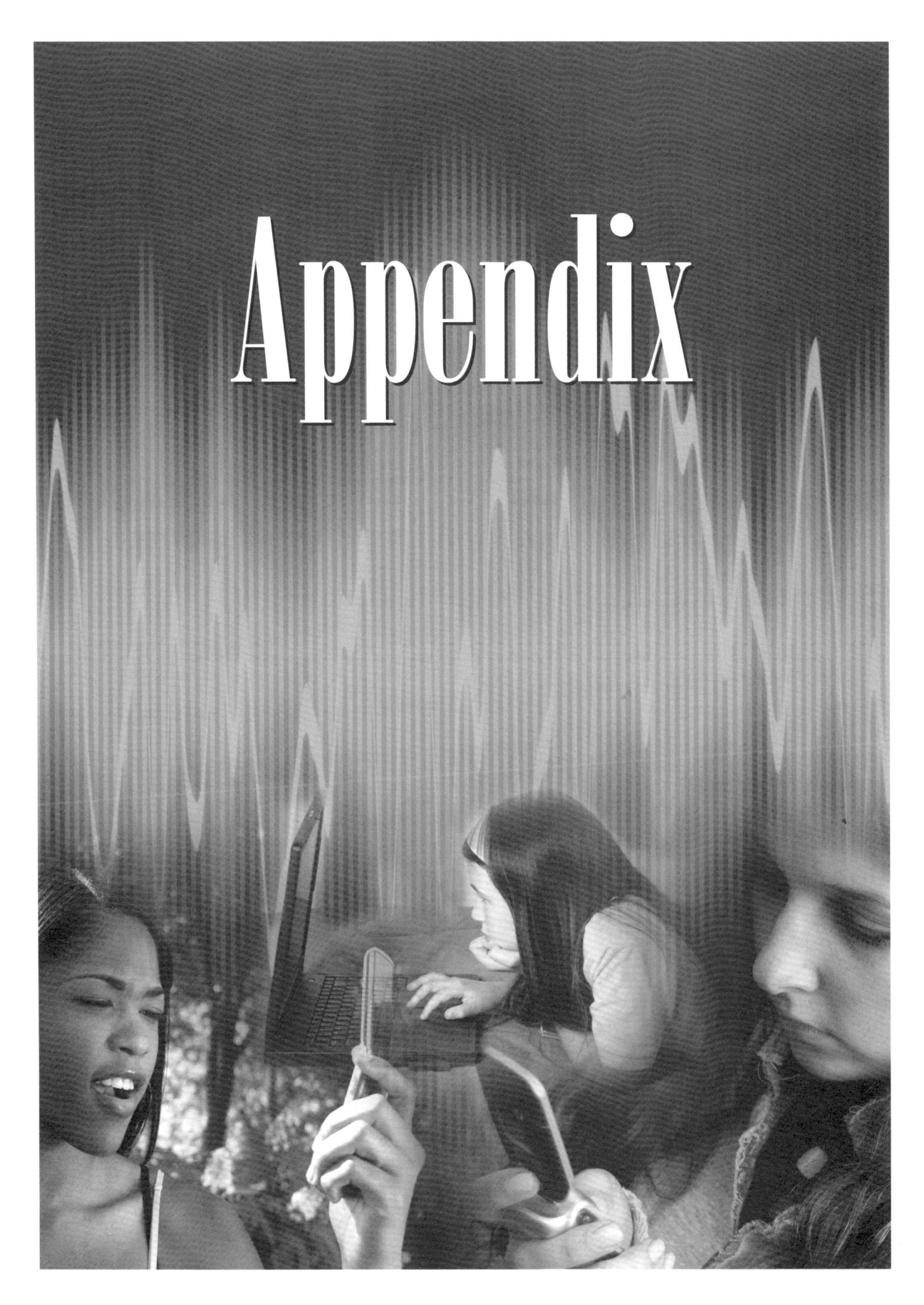

© 2009 Allyson Bowen, LISW-CP

Qualities, Strengths, Characteristics

A
Able
Accepting
Adventurous
Appreciative
Artistic
Assertive
Athletic

B
Bold
Brave
Bright

C
Calm
Caring
Cautious
Cheerful
Civile
Clever
Confident
Compassionate
Considerate
Controlled
Cooperative
Courageous
Courteous
Creative
Curious

D
Dedicated
Dependable
Determined
Devoted
Dignity
Diplomatic
Disciplined

E
Eager
Efficient
Empathetic
Encouraging
Energetic
Enthusiastic

F
Fair
Faithful
Flexible
Forgiving
Friendly
Fun-Loving

G
Generous
Gentle
Giving
Good Sport
Grateful

H
Hard Worker
Helpful
Honest
Honorable
Humble
Humorous

I
Independent
Insightful
Inspirational
Integrity
Interested
Inventive
Involved

J
Just

K
Kind

L
Laidback
Lawful
Leader
Likable
Listening
Loving
Loyal

M
Mannerly
Masterful
Mature
Merit
Moral
Motivated

© 2009 Allyson Bowen, LISW-CP

Qualities, Strengths, Characteristics

N
Neat
Noble
Nurturing

O
Obedient
Observant
On Task
Open-minded
Optimistic
Organized
Orderly

P
Patient
Patriotic
Peaceful
Perceptive
Persevering
Polite
Positive
Prepared
Pride
Principles
Punctual

Q
Quality
Quiet

R
Rational
Reasonable
Regard
Reliable
Resolute
Resourceful
Respectful
Responsible

S
Sacrificing
Self-Aware
Sensitive
Sharing
Sincere
Special
Sportmanship
Supportive
Survivalist
Sympathetic

T
Team Player
Temperate
Thoughtful
Thrifty
Tolerant
Trustworthy
Truthful

U
Understanding
Unique
Unselfish

V
Victorious
Valued
Volunteer
Valiant
Valor
Veracity

W
Warm
Watchful
Welcoming
Witty
Worker
Worthy

X
(e)xcellence

Y
Yourself

Z
Zest
Zany

National Volunteer Organizations

Many of these organizations will allow teens to volunteer. Check their website or your local chapter.

AMERICAN RED CROSS:
School-Related Activities. We fundraise, organize blood drives, provide international assistance, and learn about issues like disaster preparedness and HIV/AIDS prevention and education. www.redcrossyouth.org/volunteer

BIG BROTHERS, BIG SISTERS:
Largest and most effective youth mentoring organization in the United States. www.bbbsa.org

HABITAT FOR HUMANITY:
founded on the conviction that every man, woman and child should have a decent, safe and affordable place to live. We build with people in need regardless of race or religion. www.habit.org

LITERACY VOLUNTEERS IN AMERICA:
ProLiteracy champions the power of literacy to improve the lives of adults and their families, communities, and societies. We envision a world in which everyone can read, write, compute, and use technology to lead healthy, productive, and fulfilling lives. www.proliteracy.org

MARCH OF DIMES:
The leading nonprofit organization for pregnancy and baby health. www.marchofdimes.com or visit my personal site at www.marchforbabies.org/hudsenshope1

© 2009 Allyson Bowen, LISW-CP

National Volunteer Organizations

NATIONAL BREAST CANCER FOUNDATION:
www.Nationalbreastcancer.org

PENNIES FOR PEACE:
Educates children about the world beyond their experience and shows they can have a positive affect on a global scale, one penny at a time.
www.PenniesforPeace.org

POINTS OF LIGHT INSTITUTE:
A powerful, integrated national organization with a global focus to redefine volunteerism and civic engagement for the twenty-first century, putting people at the center of community problem solving. www.pointsoflight.org

SPECIAL OLYMPICS:
A global nonprofit organization serving the nearly 200 million people with intellectual disabilities, with a presence in nearly 200 countries worldwide.
http://www.specialolympics.org/volunteers.aspx

UNITED WAY:
http://www.liveunited.org/volunteer

VOLUNTEER MATCH:
strengthens communities by making it easier for good people and good causes to connect. www.Volunteermatch.org

© 2009 Allyson Bowen, LISW-CP

LvOL Lessons from each Activity

Inclusion: We all Belong! We all belong in the sisterhood, living, learning and loving ourselves and each other!

Current Mood: Become in tune with your "current mood" and consider how it could affect your interactions with others.

Livin' Out Loud: You came into this world to live out loud, now live it responsibly in the real world and cyber world!

Face it: Fiction, Fear, Fact?: In your everyday interactions with others pause, reflect and decide if what you think you know about someone is based on Fiction, Fear or Fact.

Cyber World: You are responsible for your electronic use! Be accountable for every "click" or "send"!

Cyber Crossword: Use your new found "techno" knowledge to be an internet savvy citizen.

A-Z Power Me! Word Find: Keep your "Power Me" list close by and practice living out loud A-Z!

'I' Card: Put the Eye Card on your computer. Commit to the "I" statements every time you use your computer.

Avatar or Who you Are?: Check in daily with yourself to see if you are wearing a mask or practicing being authentically you!

LvOL Lessons from each Activity

Me IRL: Be who you are! Be "Me IRL!" Practice daily using the characteristics and strengths from your Me IRL page.

Bullycide: Commit to step up and help someone who may be suffering. Identify who you will help and the steps you will take to help them.

She is...: Look up to your role model and recognize you can embody her same qualities. Practice implementing the qualities you listed about her.

Pieces of Me: You were pieced together to be uniquely you! Use the Pieces of Me puzzle as a visual daily reminder of the strengths and gifts you have been given to contribute positively in your relationships and interactions with others.

Guess Who: You shine when you know who you are and love the star qualities within you!

Mobile Me: Everywhere you go and everything you do let it reflect the genuine you!

Circle of Influence: Walk daily in the truth of what you believe! Surround yourself with others who have the same morals and values as you!

Hi-5: When you celebrate others you celebrate the greatest gift within you!

Media Madness: Do not be influenced by the mixed messages you receive from the media.

© 2009 Allyson Bowen, LISW-CP

LvOL Lessons from each Activity

Masterpiece: You are a masterpiece! An outstanding, beautiful work of art!

Acting Up: Practice solutions for coping with aggression in your daily interactions with others. "Act Up" to keep your interactions positive.

When Pretty in Pink turns Mean and Green: Do not let jealousy creep up on you. Live "pretty in pink" powered by you!

Kindness Cures: Give back daily. It doesn't have to be big, it starts with a simple hello, a smile or making someone feel special or welcome. Inspire!

Healing the Hurt: Live consciously in the power of forgiveness!

I Will Never: Live everyday with honor, respect, truth and love for yourself and others! Never have regrets!

Ready for Business: You have power, now you are ready for business! Walk daily in the acknowledgment of who you are, loving that person and possessing the ability to step out and shine! Go forth and do good! "be.love.do"

References

Aftab, Parry. Cyberbullying Retireved February 09, 2009 from
http://www.wiredsafety.org/cyberstalking_harassment/cyberbullying.html

Baumeister, Roy. (2002). Rejection massively reduces IQ. Retrieved May 20,2007 from www.newscientist.com

Bearman,Peter & Moody, James. (2004). Friendships play key role in suicidal thoughts of girls, but not boys. Retrieved September 12,2007 from www.psychport.com

Bregndon, Mara, Boivin, M., Dionne G., Girard, A., Perusse, D., Vitaro, F. (2005). Examining Genetic and Environmental Effects on Social Aggression: A Study of 6-Year-Old Twins. Child Development, 76, 4.

Bullywatch. Stories. Retrieved March 30, 2009, from http://www.bullywatch.org/victims_stories.html

Centers for Disease Control and Prevention. Surveillance Summaries, May 21, 2004. MMWR 2004:53 (No. SS-2).

Christina Aguilera. Retrieved March 29, 2009, from http://www.christinamultimedia.com/statistics/didyouknow.php

Crick, N. & Grotpeter, J. (1995). Relational Aggression, gender and social psychological adjustment. Child Development, 66, 710-722.

Eva Longoria. Retrieved March 29, 2009 from
www.dailymail.co.uk/tvshowbiz/article-511229/How-I-bullied-ugly-Eva-Longoria.html

Girls Inc.,The Supergirl Dilemma: Girls Feel the Pressure to be Perfect, Accomplished, Thin, and Accommodating. Retrieved May 20, 2007, from www.girlsinc.org

Goleman, Daniel. How Emotions Matter for Health. Retrieved August 18, 2007, from www.kidseq.com

"Her teen committed suicide over "sexting." Today Show. National Broadcast Company. WIS, Columbia, SC. 6 Mar. 2009.

Hertz, M.F., David-Ferdon, C. (2008) Electronic Media and Youth Violence: A CDC Issue Brief for Educators and Caregivers. Atlanta (GA): Centers for Disease Control.

Kowalski, R., Limber, S., Agatston, P. (2008). Cyber Bullying: Bullying in the Digital Age. Oxford, UK: Blackwell Publishing.

Marr, N. & Field, T. (2001). Bullycide: Death at Playtime, An Expose of Child Suicide Caused by Bullying. UK; Success Unlimited.

Merrian Webster Online. http://www.merriam-webster.com/

Miley Cyrus. Retrieved March 29, 2009, from http://www.popcrunch.com/miley-cyrus-bullied/

Simmons, R. (2002). Odd girl out: The hidden culture of aggression in girls. SanDiego, CA: Harcourt Trade Publishing.

The National Campaign and CosmoGirl.com Reveal Results of Sex & Tech Survey. Retrieved March 03, 2009, from http://www.thenationalcampaign.org/media/press-release.aspx?releaseID=23

US Magazine. Celebs who were Bullied. Retrieved March 29, 2009, from http://www.usmagazine.com/celebs-who-were-bullied

Webopedia. www.webopedia.com

About the Author

Allyson Bowen, LISW-CP is a Licensed Clinical Social Worker in clinical private practice and is co-owner and director of Turning Point Counseling in West Columbia, SC. She focuses on educating "tweens", teens and women about female relational issues and challenges. Allyson developed a Relational Aggression Survey used in schools throughout the US and Canada to identify female bullying behaviors in girl's grades 3-12. She is also co-author of the book, Mean Girls: 101½ Creative Strategies and Activities for Working with Relational Aggression.

Allyson is a renowned speaker and national consultant on relational aggression and bullying. She has led professional seminars and worked with youth across the US and Canada on topics such as: relational aggression, anger, bullying, cyber-bullying, peer relationships and adolescent behaviors and disorders. She is also a member of the International Bullying Prevention Association.

In addition, Allyson is a past adjunct professor at Limestone College, South Carolinas largest private accredited institution. She served in the Social Work Department focusing on human behavior, sexuality and gender role differences.

Allyson volunteers speaking to community/civic groups educating them about relational aggression/bullying and encouraging mentorship/volunteerism with youth. In addition, she works to educate parents about the daily perils of peer relationships their children face in school.

Allyson received her BA in Social Work from Columbia College and her Masters degree in Social Work from the University of South Carolina.

Allyson is married to her high school sweetheart Eric and they have one son, Asher.

Allyson's high energy and humor challenges and motivates audiences in making positive changes in their work. She educates, entertains and leaves everyone inspired with her wit and wisdom.